MW01272887

Blackstone Outdoor Gas Griddle Cookbook for Beginners

1000 Days of Easy and Quick, Simple & Delicious Gas Griddle Recipes to Master Your Grill with a picture.

By Dr. Paula

TABLE OF CONTENTS

Welcome to the world of outdoor griddling with the Blackstone Outdoor Gas Griddle Cookbook for Beginners! Whether you're a seasoned griller looking to expand your repertoire or a complete novice eager to embark on a flavorful journey, you've come to the right place. In this cookbook, we'll guide you through 1000 days of easy, quick, and delicious recipes specifically crafted for your Blackstone Outdoor Gas Griddle.

Griddling isn't just about cooking food; it's about creating memorable experiences with family and friends, enjoying the great outdoors, and savouring mouthwatering meals that tantalize the taste buds. With the versatility and convenience of your Blackstone grill, the possibilities are endless. From breakfast classics to gourmet dinners and everything in between, you'll find a wealth of inspiration to elevate your outdoor cooking game.

We understand that mastering a new cooking appliance can be daunting, so we've tailored this cookbook with beginners in mind. Each recipe is accompanied by step-by-step instructions and handy tips to ensure your griddling experience is as effortless and enjoyable as possible. Whether you're firing up the grill for a weekend brunch, a backyard barbecue, or a cosy dinner under the stars, you'll feel confident and empowered to create culinary masterpieces that impress even the toughest critics.

So, dust off your Blackstone Outdoor Gas Griddle, gather your ingredients, and prepare for a delicious adventure. With the Blackstone Outdoor Gas Griddle Cookbook for Beginners as your guide, you'll soon be griddling like a pro and delighting your taste buds with every bite.

FLUFFY PANCAKES

Prep Time: 10 minutes

Cooking Time: 10 minutes

Servings: 4

Ingredients:

- 1 1/2 cups all-purpose flour
- 3 1/2 teaspoons baking powder
- one teaspoon salt
- one tablespoon white sugar
- 1 1/4 cups milk
- one egg
- three tablespoons butter, melted

Directions:

1. sift together the flour, baking powder, salt, and sugar in a large bowl.

2. Make a well in the centre and pour in the milk, egg, and melted butter; mix until smooth.

3. Heat a lightly oiled griddle or frying pan over medium-high heat.

4. Pour or scoop the batter onto the griddle, using approximately 1/4 cup for each pancake.

5. Cook until bubbles form and the edges are golden, then flip and cook until browned on the other side.

6. Repeat with the remaining batter.

7. Serve hot with your favourite toppings such as maple syrup, fresh fruits, or whipped cream.

Nutrition Facts (per serving):

- Calories: 256
- Total Fat: 9g

- Saturated Fat: 5g
- Cholesterol: 59mg
- Sodium: 818mg
- Total Carbohydrate: 36g
- Dietary Fiber: 1g
- Sugars: 5g
- Protein: 7g

Classic French Toast

Prep Time: 10 minutes

Cooking Time: 10 minutes

Servings: 4

Ingredients:

- eight slices of thick-cut bread (such as brioche or challah)
- four large eggs
- 1 cup whole milk
- one teaspoon vanilla extract
- two tablespoons granulated sugar
- 1/2 teaspoon ground cinnamon
- Butter or oil for cooking
- Maple syrup, powdered sugar, and fresh berries for serving (optional)

Directions:

1. Preheat griddle or skillet: Heat a griddle or large skillet over medium heat. Grease lightly with butter or oil.

2. Prepare egg mixture: In a shallow dish, whisk together eggs, milk, vanilla extract, sugar, and cinnamon until well combined.

3. Soak bread slices: Dip each slice of bread into the egg mixture, ensuring both sides are coated evenly. Allow excess egg mixture to drip off.

4. Cook French toast: Place the soaked bread slices onto the preheated griddle or skillet. Cook for 2-3 minutes on each side until golden brown is cooked through.

5. Serve: Transfer the cooked French toast to plates. If desired, serve warm with maple syrup, powdered sugar, and fresh berries.

Nutrition Facts (per serving):

• Calories: 320 kcal

• Fat: 12g

• Saturated Fat: 4g

• Cholesterol: 195mg

• Sodium: 400mg

• Carbohydrates: 41g

• Fiber: 2g

• Sugars: 10g

• Protein: 12g

BREAKFAST BURRITOS

• Prep Time: 15 minutes

• Cooking Time: 15 minutes

• Servings: 4

Ingredients:

• four large flour tortillas

• eight large eggs

• 1 cup diced cooked ham or breakfast sausage

• 1 cup shredded cheddar cheese

• 1/2 cup diced bell peppers (any colour)

• 1/4 cup diced onion

• Salt and pepper to taste

• two tablespoons olive oil

• Salsa and sour cream for serving (optional)

Directions:

1. Heat olive oil over medium heat in a large skillet. Add diced bell peppers and onions. Sauté until they begin to soften, about 3-4 minutes.

2. Add diced ham or breakfast sausage to the skillet. Cook until heated through, about 2-3 minutes.

3. In a bowl, beat the eggs and season with salt and pepper. Pour the beaten eggs into the skillet with the other ingredients.

4. Gently scramble the eggs with the ham or sausage, peppers, and onions until cooked through but still moist. Remove from heat.

5. Warm the flour tortillas in a separate skillet or microwave.

6. Divide the egg mixture evenly among the tortillas, placing it in the centre of each one.

7. Sprinkle shredded cheddar cheese over the egg mixture on each tortilla.

8. Fold the sides of the tortillas over the filling, then roll them up tightly to form burritos.

9. Place the burritos seam-side down on a plate or serving dish.

10. Optionally, you can wrap each burrito in foil to keep them warm.

11. Serve the breakfast burritos with salsa and sour cream on the side, if desired.

Nutrition Facts (per serving):

• Calories: 410

• Total Fat: 24g

• Saturated Fat: 9g

• Cholesterol: 380mg

• Sodium: 730mg

• Total Carbohydrates: 26g

• Dietary Fiber: 2g

• Sugars: 2g

• Protein: 23g

VEGGIE OMELETTE

• Prep Time: 10 minutes

• Cooking Time: 10 minutes

• Servings: 2

Ingredients:

- four large eggs
- 1/4 cup diced bell peppers (any colour)
- 1/4 cup diced tomatoes
- 1/4 cup chopped spinach
- 1/4 cup diced onions
- Salt and pepper to taste
- one tablespoon olive oil
- 1/4 cup shredded cheese (optional)

Directions:

1. In a bowl, whisk the eggs until well beaten. Season with salt and pepper according to your taste.

2. Heat olive oil in a non-stick skillet over medium heat.

3. Add diced onions and sauté until translucent.

4. Add bell peppers and tomatoes to the skillet. Cook for 2-3 minutes until they start to soften.

5. Add chopped spinach to the skillet and cook for another 1-2 minutes until wilted.

6. Pour the beaten eggs over the vegetables in the skillet. Allow the eggs to cook undisturbed for a minute.

7. Gently lift the edges of the omelette with a spatula, allowing any uncooked egg to flow underneath.

8. Once the omelette is mostly set but still slightly runny on top, sprinkle shredded cheese over one-half of the omelette if using.

9. Carefully fold the omelette in half with a spatula.

10. Cook for another 1-2 minutes until the cheese is melted and the omelette is cooked.

11. Slide the omelette onto a plate and serve hot.

Nutrition Facts (per serving):

- Calories: 215
- Total Fat: 15g
- Saturated Fat: 4g

- Cholesterol: 372mg
- Sodium: 275mg
- Total Carbohydrates: 7g
- Dietary Fiber: 2g
- Sugars: 3g
- Protein: 14g

BLUEBERRY PANCAKES

Prep Time: 10 minutes

Cooking Time: 15 minutes

Servings: 4

Ingredients:

- 1 1/2 cups all-purpose flour
- 3 1/2 teaspoons baking powder
- one teaspoon salt
- one tablespoon white sugar
- 1 1/4 cups milk
- one egg
- three tablespoons melted butter
- 1 cup fresh blueberries
- Butter or oil for cooking

Directions:

1. Mix Dry Ingredients: In a large bowl, sift together the flour, baking powder, salt, and sugar.

2. Combine Wet Ingredients: In another bowl, beat the milk, egg, and melted butter until well combined.

3. Combine Dry and Wet Ingredients: Pour the wet ingredients into the dry ingredients and stir until combined. Do not overmix; a few lumps are okay.

4. Fold in Blueberries: Gently fold the blueberries into the batter.

5. Heat Pan: Heat a non-stick skillet or griddle over medium heat and add a small amount of butter or oil to coat the surface.

6. Cook Pancakes: Pour about 1/4 cup of batter onto the skillet for each pancake. Cook until bubbles form on the surface and the edges start to look set, about 2-3 minutes.

7. Flip and Cook: Flip the pancakes and cook until golden brown on the other side, about 1-2 minutes more.

8. Serve the pancakes warm with maple syrup and extra blueberries if desired.

Nutrition Facts (per serving):

• Calories: 300

• Total Fat: 10g

• Saturated Fat: 6g

• Cholesterol: 65mg

• Sodium: 700mg

• Total Carbohydrate: 45g

• Dietary Fiber: 2g

• Sugars: 8g

• Protein: 8g

BACON AND EGG BREAKFAST SANDWICHES

Prep Time: 10 minutes

Cooking Time: 10 minutes

Servings: 2

Ingredients:

• four slices of bacon

• two large eggs

• four slices of your favourite bread (such as ciabatta or whole wheat)

• two slices of cheese (cheddar, Swiss, or your preference)

• two teaspoons butter

• Salt and pepper to taste

• Optional toppings: lettuce, tomato, avocado

Directions:

1. Cook Bacon: Cook the bacon in a skillet over medium heat until crispy. Remove it from the skillet and drain on paper towels.

2. Cook Eggs: In the same skillet, discard excess bacon grease, leaving about a teaspoon in the skillet. Crack the eggs into the skillet and cook to your desired doneness, seasoning with salt and pepper. For a classic sandwich, cook until the yolks are still slightly runny.

3. Toast Bread: While cooking eggs, toast the bread slices in a toaster or on a separate skillet until golden brown.

4. Assemble Sandwiches: Spread butter on one side of each slice of toasted bread. Place a slice of cheese on the unbuttered side of two slices of bread. Top with cooked bacon, followed by the cooked eggs. Add any optional toppings if desired. Finish with the remaining slices of bread, buttered side facing out.

5. Serve: Slice the sandwiches in half and serve immediately while warm.

Nutrition Facts (per serving):

• Calories: 420

• Total Fat: 25g

• Saturated Fat: 10g

• Trans Fat: 0g

• Cholesterol: 250mg

• Sodium: 740mg

• Total Carbohydrates: 26g

• Dietary Fiber: 2g

• Sugars: 2g

• Protein: 23g

SAUSAGE BREAKFAST HASH

Prep Time: 10 minutes

Cooking Time: 20 minutes

Servings: 4

Ingredients:

• 1 lb (450g) breakfast sausage

- four medium potatoes, diced
- one onion, diced
- one red bell pepper, diced
- one green bell pepper, diced
- two cloves garlic, minced
- one teaspoon paprika
- one teaspoon dried thyme
- Salt and pepper to taste
- four eggs (optional)
- Chopped fresh parsley for garnish

Directions:

1. Cook Sausage: In a large skillet over medium heat, cook the breakfast sausage until browned and cooked through, breaking it up into smaller pieces with a spatula as it cooks. Remove the sausage from the skillet and set aside, leaving the rendered fat in the skillet.

2. Cook Potatoes: Add the diced potatoes to the same skillet with the rendered fat. Cook, stirring occasionally, until the potatoes are golden brown and cooked through about 10-12 minutes.

3. Add Vegetables: Add the diced onion, bell peppers, and minced garlic to the skillet with the potatoes. Cook, stirring occasionally, until the vegetables are tender, about 5 minutes.

4. Season: Sprinkle the paprika, dried thyme, salt, and pepper over the sausage and vegetable mixture. Stir well to combine and cook for another 2-3 minutes to allow the flavours to meld together.

5. Optional Eggs: If desired, create wells in the hash mixture and crack an egg into each well. Cover the skillet and cook until the eggs are done to your liking, about 4-5 minutes for runny yolks or longer for firmer yolks.

6. Serve: Once the eggs are cooked (if using), sprinkle chopped fresh parsley over the hash. Serve hot, straight from the skillet.

Nutrition Facts (per serving):

- Calories: 420
- Total Fat: 26g
- Saturated Fat: 9g

- Cholesterol: 240mg
- Sodium: 780mg
- Total Carbohydrate: 25g
- Dietary Fiber: 4g
- Sugars: 3g
- Protein: 22g

CINNAMON ROLL PANCAKES

Prep Time: 15 minutes

Cooking Time: 20 minutes

Servings: 4

Ingredients:

- For the Pancake Batter:
- 1 1/2 cups all-purpose flour
- one tablespoon baking powder
- one tablespoon granulated sugar
- 1/4 teaspoon salt
- 1 cup milk
- one large egg
- two tablespoons melted butter
- For the Cinnamon Filling:
- 1/4 cup unsalted butter, softened
- 1/4 cup brown sugar
- one tablespoon ground cinnamon
- For the Cream Cheese Glaze:
- 4 ounces cream cheese, softened
- 1 cup powdered sugar
- one teaspoon vanilla extract
- 2-3 tablespoons milk

Directions:

1. Prepare the Pancake Batter: In a mixing bowl, whisk together the flour, baking powder, sugar, and salt. Whisk together the milk, egg, and melted butter in another bowl. Pour the wet ingredients into the dry ingredients and mix until just combined. Set aside.

2. Make the Cinnamon Filling: In a small bowl, combine the softened butter, brown sugar, and ground cinnamon. Mix until smooth and well combined. Transfer the mixture to a piping or plastic sandwich bag with a small corner snipped off. Set aside.

3. Cook the Pancakes: Heat a non-stick skillet or griddle over medium heat and lightly grease with butter or cooking spray. Pour about 1/4 cup of pancake batter onto the skillet for each pancake. Once bubbles start to form on the surface, pipe a spiral of the cinnamon filling onto each pancake. Cook for another 1-2 minutes; flip the pancakes and cook until golden brown on the other side. Remove from the skillet and repeat with the remaining batter and filling.

4. Prepare the Cream Cheese Glaze: In a mixing bowl, beat together the softened cream cheese, powdered sugar, vanilla extract, and enough milk to achieve a smooth, pourable consistency.

5. Serve: Drizzle the cream cheese glaze over the warm cinnamon roll pancakes and serve immediately.

Nutrition Facts (per serving):

• Calories: 520

• Total Fat: 24g

• Saturated Fat: 15g

• Cholesterol: 110mg

• Sodium: 540mg

• Total Carbohydrate: 68g

• Dietary Fiber: 2g

• Sugars: 35g

• Protein: 9g

BREAKFAST QUESADILLAS

Prep Time: 10 minutes

Cooking Time: 10 minutes

Servings: 4

Ingredients:

• four large flour tortillas

• six large eggs, beaten

• 1 cup shredded cheddar cheese

• 1 cup cooked and crumbled breakfast sausage or bacon

• 1/2 cup diced bell peppers

• 1/4 cup diced onions

• Salt and pepper to taste

• Optional toppings: salsa, sour cream, avocado slices

Directions:

1. In a large skillet over medium heat, cook the breakfast sausage or bacon until browned and cooked. Remove from the skillet and set aside.

2. add a little oil, if needed, in the same skillet and sauté the diced bell peppers and onions until they are softened, about 3-4 minutes. Remove from heat and set aside.

3. In a separate skillet, scramble the eggs until they are cooked but still slightly moist. Season with salt and pepper to taste.

4. Lay out the flour tortillas on a clean surface. Divide the scrambled eggs, cooked sausage or bacon, sautéed bell peppers, and onions evenly among the tortillas.

5. Sprinkle shredded cheddar cheese over the top of each tortilla.

6. Fold each tortilla in half, pressing down gently to seal.

7. Heat a large skillet or griddle over medium heat. Cook the quesadillas on each side for 2-3 minutes or until they are golden brown and the cheese is melted.

8. Remove from heat and let cool for a minute before slicing into wedges.

9. Serve hot with optional toppings such as salsa, sour cream, or avocado slices.

Nutrition Facts (per serving):

• Calories: 380

- Total Fat: 23g
- Saturated Fat: 10g
- Cholesterol: 295mg
- Sodium: 680mg
- Total Carbohydrates: 22g
- Dietary Fiber: 2g
- Sugars: 2g
- Protein: 21g

BANANA NUT WAFFLES

Prep Time: 15 minutes

Cooking Time: 15 minutes

Servings: 4

Ingredients:

- two ripe bananas, mashed
- 2 cups all-purpose flour
- one tablespoon baking powder
- 1/4 teaspoon salt
- two tablespoons granulated sugar
- two large eggs
- 1 1/2 cups milk
- 1/4 cup vegetable oil
- one teaspoon vanilla extract
- 1/2 cup chopped walnuts or pecans

Directions:

1. Combine the mashed bananas, flour, baking powder, salt, and sugar in a large mixing bowl.

2. whisk together eggs, milk, vegetable oil, and vanilla extract until well combined.

3. Pour the wet ingredients into the dry ingredients and stir until combined. Fold in the chopped nuts.

4. Preheat your waffle iron and lightly grease it with non-stick cooking spray.

5. Pour enough batter onto the hot waffle iron to cover the waffle grid. Close the lid and cook according to the manufacturer's instructions or until golden brown and crisp.

6. Remove the waffle carefully and repeat with the remaining batter.

7. Serve warm with your favourite toppings, such as sliced bananas, chopped nuts, maple syrup, or whipped cream.

Nutrition Facts (per serving):

• Calories: 472

• Total Fat: 20g

• Saturated Fat: 3g

• Trans Fat: 0g

• Cholesterol: 93mg

• Sodium: 393mg

• Total Carbohydrates: 61g

• Dietary Fiber: 3g

• Sugars: 15g

• Protein: 13g

Breakfast Skillet

Prep Time: 10 minutes

Cooking Time: 20 minutes

Servings: 4

Ingredients:

• four large eggs

• four slices of bacon, chopped

• 2 cups diced potatoes

• one small onion, diced

• one bell pepper, diced

- 1 cup shredded cheddar cheese
- Salt and pepper to taste
- two tablespoons olive oil
- Optional toppings: chopped green onions, hot sauce

Directions:

1. Preheat olive oil in a large skillet over medium heat.

2. Cook Bacon: Add chopped bacon to the skillet and cook until crisp. Remove bacon from the skillet and set aside, leaving the bacon fat in the skillet.

3. Cook Potatoes: Add diced potatoes in the same skillet with the bacon fat. Cook until golden brown and crispy, stirring occasionally, about 10-12 minutes.

4. Add Vegetables: Add diced onion and bell pepper to the skillet with the potatoes. Cook until vegetables are softened, about 3-4 minutes.

5. Combine Ingredients: Once the vegetables are cooked, return the cooked bacon to the skillet and stir to combine.

6. Crack Eggs: Add four wells in the potato mixture and add an egg to each.

7. Cook Eggs: Cover the skillet and cook until the eggs are set to your liking, about 5-7 minutes for runny yolks or longer for firmer yolks.

8. Add Cheese: Sprinkle shredded cheddar cheese over the skillet during the last 2 minutes of cooking.

9. Serve: Remove the skillet from heat once the cheese is melted and the eggs are cooked to your preference. Season with salt and pepper to taste.

10. Garnish: Garnish with chopped green onions and serve hot with optional hot sauce.

Nutrition Facts (per serving):

- Calories: 385
- Total Fat: 26g
- Saturated Fat: 9g
- Cholesterol: 228mg
- Sodium: 472mg
- Total Carbohydrate: 20g
- Dietary Fiber: 2g

- Sugars: 3g
- Protein: 18g

BREAKFAST TACOS

Prep Time: 10 minutes

Cooking Time: 15 minutes

Servings: 4

Ingredients:

- eight small flour tortillas
- eight large eggs
- 1 cup diced tomatoes
- 1 cup cooked and crumbled breakfast sausage
- 1 cup shredded cheddar cheese
- one avocado, sliced
- 1/2 cup chopped fresh cilantro
- Salt and pepper to taste
- Salsa, for serving
- Sour cream for serving

Directions:

1. In a large skillet, cook the breakfast sausage over medium heat until browned and cooked. Remove from skillet and set aside.

2. Crack the eggs and scramble them until fully cooked in the same skillet. Season with salt and pepper to taste.

3. Warm the tortillas in a separate skillet or microwave until soft and pliable.

4. Assemble the tacos by spooning scrambled eggs onto each tortilla. Top with diced tomatoes, cooked breakfast sausage, shredded cheese, avocado slices, and chopped cilantro.

5. Serve the breakfast tacos warm with salsa and sour cream on the side.

Nutrition Facts (per serving):

- Calories: 420
- Total Fat: 24g

- Saturated Fat: 9g
- Cholesterol: 320mg
- Sodium: 620mg
- Total Carbohydrates: 28g
- Dietary Fiber: 6g
- Sugars: 3g
- Protein: 24g

GREEK YOGURT PARFAIT

Prep Time: 10 minutes

Cooking Time: 0 minutes

Servings: 2

Ingredients:

- 1 cup Greek yogurt
- 1/2 cup granola
- 1 cup mixed berries (strawberries, blueberries, raspberries)
- two tablespoons honey or maple syrup
- 1/4 teaspoon vanilla extract
- Fresh mint leaves for garnish (optional)

Directions:

1. In a small bowl, mix the Greek yoghurt with honey or maple syrup and vanilla extract until well combined.

2. In serving glasses or bowls, layer the ingredients starting with a spoonful of Greek yoghurt mixture at the bottom.

3. Add a layer of granola on top of the yoghurt.

4. Follow with a layer of mixed berries.

5. Repeat the layers until the glasses are filled, ending with a layer of berries on top.

6. Garnish with fresh mint leaves if desired.

7. Serve immediately or refrigerate until ready to eat.

Nutrition Facts (per serving):

• Calories: 250

• Total Fat: 6g

• Saturated Fat: 1g

• Cholesterol: 5mg

• Sodium: 50mg

• Total Carbohydrates: 38g

• Dietary Fiber: 4g

• Sugars: 22g

• Protein: 13g

BREAKFAST PIZZA

Prep Time: 15 minutes

Cooking Time: 20 minutes

Servings: 4

Ingredients:

• one pre-made pizza dough (or homemade if preferred)

• 1 cup shredded mozzarella cheese

• 1 cup cooked breakfast sausage, crumbled

• 1 cup diced bell peppers (any colour you prefer)

• ½ cup diced onions

• four large eggs

• Salt and pepper to taste

• two tablespoons chopped fresh parsley (optional, for garnish)

Directions:

1. Preheat your oven to 400°F (200°C).

2. Roll out the pizza dough onto a baking sheet lined with parchment paper.

3. Sprinkle half the shredded mozzarella cheese evenly over the pizza dough.

4. Evenly distribute the cooked breakfast sausage, diced bell peppers, and onions over the cheese.

5. Create four wells in the toppings for the eggs.

6. Carefully crack one egg into each well.

7. Season with salt and pepper to taste.

8. Sprinkle the remaining mozzarella cheese over the top.

9. Bake in the oven for 15-20 minutes or until the crust is golden brown and the egg whites are set.

10. Once cooked, remove from the oven and let it cool for a few minutes.

11. Garnish with chopped fresh parsley if desired.

12. Slice the breakfast pizza into wedges and serve hot.

Nutrition Facts (per serving):

• Calories: 380

• Total Fat: 18g

• Saturated Fat: 7g

• Cholesterol: 220mg

• Sodium: 840mg

• Total Carbohydrates: 31g

• Dietary Fiber: 2g

• Sugars: 3g

• Protein: 22g

BREAKFAST SLIDERS

Prep Time: 15 minutes

Cooking Time: 25 minutes

Servings: 12 sliders

Ingredients:

• 12 slider buns

• six large eggs

• 12 slices of cooked bacon

• 12 slices of cheddar cheese

• 1 tablespoon butter

• Salt and pepper to taste

• Optional: sliced avocado, tomato, or spinach for garnish

Directions:

1. Preheat your oven to 350°F (175°C).

2. In a large skillet, melt the butter over medium heat.

3. Crack the eggs into the skillet, season with salt and pepper, and scramble until fully cooked. Remove from heat.

4. Slice the slider buns horizontally and place the bottom halves in a baking dish.

5. Layer each bottom bun with a slice of cheddar cheese, followed by a portion of scrambled eggs, a slice of bacon, and any optional toppings.

6. Top each slider with the remaining half of the buns.

7. Cover the baking dish with aluminium foil and bake in the oven for about 15 minutes, or until the cheese is melted and the sliders are heated.

8. Remove the foil and bake for 5-10 minutes to lightly toast the buns.

9. Once done, remove from the oven and serve hot.

Nutrition Facts (per serving):

• Calories: 280

• Total Fat: 15g

• Saturated Fat: 7g

• Trans Fat: 0g

• Cholesterol: 145mg

• Sodium: 450mg

• Total Carbohydrates: 21g

• Dietary Fiber: 1g

• Sugars: 3g

• Protein: 14g

BREAKFAST FAJITAS

Prep Time: 15 minutes

Cooking Time: 15 minutes

Servings: 4

Ingredients:

- eight large eggs
- 1 tablespoon olive oil
- one bell pepper, thinly sliced
- one onion, thinly sliced
- 1 cup cooked black beans
- 1 cup cooked diced potatoes
- 1 cup shredded cheddar cheese
- eight small flour tortillas
- Salt and pepper to taste
- Optional toppings: salsa, avocado slices, sour cream, chopped cilantro

Directions:

1. Heat olive oil over medium heat in a large skillet. Add sliced bell pepper and onion and sauté until softened, about 5 minutes.

2. Push the vegetables to one side of the skillet and crack the eggs into the other. Scramble the eggs until cooked through, then mix with the vegetables.

3. Add cooked black beans and diced potatoes to the skillet, stirring until heated.

4. Warm the flour tortillas in a separate skillet or microwave.

5. Place a scoop of the egg and vegetable mixture onto each tortilla, then sprinkle with shredded cheddar cheese.

6. Serve hot with optional toppings like salsa, avocado slices, sour cream, and chopped cilantro.

Nutrition Facts (per serving):

- Calories: 395
- Total Fat: 19g
- Saturated Fat: 7g
- Cholesterol: 373mg
- Sodium: 535mg
- Total Carbohydrate: 36g

- Dietary Fiber: 5g
- Sugars: 3g
- Protein: 20g

Avocado Toast with Poached Eggs

Prep Time: 10 minutes

Cooking Time: 5 minutes

Servings: 2

Ingredients:

- two ripe avocados
- four slices of whole-grain bread
- 4 eggs
- one tablespoon white vinegar
- Salt and pepper to taste
- Optional toppings: cherry tomatoes, feta cheese, red pepper flakes, chopped cilantro

Directions:

1. Prepare Avocado Spread:

- Cut the avocados in half, remove the pits, and scoop the flesh into a bowl.
- Mash the avocado with a fork until smooth but still slightly chunky.
- Season with salt and pepper to taste.

2. Toast the Bread:

- Toast the slices of whole grain bread until golden brown and crispy.

3. Poach the Eggs:

- Fill a large saucepan with water and bring it to a gentle simmer over medium heat.
- Add the vinegar to the water.
- Crack each egg into a small bowl.
- Carefully slide the eggs, one at a time, into the simmering water.
- Poach the eggs for about 3-4 minutes until the whites are set, but the yolks are still runny.

• Remove the poached eggs from the water using a slotted spoon and drain them on a paper towel.

4. Assemble the Avocado Toast:

• Spread a generous amount of mashed avocado onto each slice of toasted bread.

• Place a poached egg on top of the avocado spread.

• Season the eggs with salt and pepper.

5. Add Optional Toppings:

• Sprinkle with optional toppings such as cherry tomatoes, crumbled feta cheese, red pepper flakes, or chopped cilantro for extra flavour and texture.

6. Serve:

• Serve the avocado toast with poached eggs immediately while still warm.

Nutrition Facts (per serving):

• Calories: 350

• Total Fat: 20g

• Saturated Fat: 3g

• Cholesterol: 185mg

• Sodium: 280mg

• Total Carbohydrates: 30g

• Dietary Fiber: 12g

• Sugars: 3g

• Protein: 14g

BREAKFAST GRILLED CHEESE

Prep Time: 10 minutes

Cooking Time: 10 minutes

Servings: 2

Ingredients:

• 4 slices of bread (whole wheat or sourdough recommended)

• four slices of cheddar cheese

- four slices of cooked bacon
- two large eggs
- two tablespoons butter
- Salt and pepper to taste
- Optional: sliced avocado, tomato, or spinach for extra fillings

Directions:

1. Cook Bacon: In a skillet over medium heat, cook the bacon until crispy. Remove from the skillet and set aside on a paper towel-lined plate to drain excess grease.

2. Prepare Eggs: In the same skillet, crack the eggs and fry them according to your preference (fried or scrambled). Season with salt and pepper. Once cooked, set aside.

3. Assemble Sandwiches: Take two slices of bread and layer each with a slice of cheddar cheese, followed by bacon slices, and then the cooked eggs. Optionally, add any extra fillings like avocado, tomato, or spinach. Top each with another slice of cheddar cheese and cover with the remaining bread slices to form sandwiches.

4. Grill Sandwiches: Melt one tablespoon of butter in a clean skillet over medium heat. Once melted, place the assembled sandwiches in the skillet. Cook for 3-4 minutes on each side until the bread is golden brown and the cheese is melted.

5. Serve: Once the sandwiches are grilled to perfection, remove them from the skillet and let them cool for a minute. Slice diagonally and serve hot.

Nutrition Facts (per serving):

Note: Nutrition facts may vary depending on the type and amount of optional ingredients used.

- Calories: 550
- Total Fat: 34g
- Saturated Fat: 17g
- Cholesterol: 275mg
- Sodium: 970mg
- Total Carbohydrates: 31g
- Dietary Fiber: 2g

- Sugars: 2g
- Protein: 29g

SPINACH AND FETA EGG MUFFINS

Prep Time: 15 minutes

Cooking Time: 20 minutes

Servings: 12 muffins

Ingredients:

- eight large eggs
- 1 cup chopped spinach
- 1/2 cup crumbled feta cheese
- 1/4 cup diced red bell pepper
- 1/4 cup diced onion
- two tablespoons chopped fresh parsley
- Salt and pepper to taste
- Cooking spray or olive oil for greasing muffin tin

Directions:

1. Preheat your oven to 350°F (175°C). Grease a 12-cup muffin tin with cooking spray or olive oil.

2. In a mixing bowl, crack the eggs and whisk until well beaten.

3. Add the chopped spinach, crumbled feta cheese, diced red bell pepper, diced onion, chopped parsley, salt, and pepper to the eggs. Stir until all ingredients are well combined.

4. Pour the egg mixture evenly into the prepared muffin tin, filling each cup about 3/4 full.

5. Bake in the oven for 18-20 minutes until the egg muffins are set and lightly golden on top.

6. Remove the muffin tin from the oven and let the egg muffins cool for a few minutes before carefully removing them from the tin.

7. Serve warm and enjoy!

Nutrition Facts (per serving):

- Calories: 89
- Total Fat: 6g
- Saturated Fat: 2.6g
- Cholesterol: 154mg
- Sodium: 136mg
- Total Carbohydrates: 1.5g
- Dietary Fiber: 0.3g
- Total Sugars: 0.7g
- Protein: 7.4g

BREAKFAST STUFFED PEPPERS

Prep Time: 15 minutes

Cooking Time: 25 minutes

Servings: 4

Ingredients:

- four large bell peppers (any colour), halved and seeds removed
- eight eggs
- 1 cup cooked quinoa
- 1 cup cooked turkey sausage, crumbled
- 1/2 cup diced onion
- 1/2 cup diced bell peppers (any colour)
- 1 cup shredded cheddar cheese
- Salt and pepper to taste
- Chopped fresh parsley for garnish (optional)

Directions:

1. Preheat your oven to 375°F (190°C).

2. Place the halved bell peppers in a baking dish, cut side up, and set aside.

3. In a mixing bowl, whisk the eggs until well beaten.

4. Stir in the cooked quinoa, turkey sausage, diced onion, diced bell peppers, and half of the shredded cheddar cheese. Season with salt and pepper to taste.

5. Spoon the egg mixture into each bell pepper half until evenly filled.

6. Sprinkle the remaining shredded cheddar cheese on each stuffed pepper.

7. Cover the baking dish with foil and bake in the oven for 20 minutes.

8. Remove the foil and bake for 5-7 minutes until the eggs are set and the cheese is melted and bubbly.

9. Once done, remove from the oven and let cool for a few minutes before serving.

10. Garnish with chopped fresh parsley if desired, then serve and enjoy!

Nutrition Facts (per serving):

• Calories: 348 kcal

• Total Fat: 19g

• Saturated Fat: 8g

• Cholesterol: 394mg

• Sodium: 499mg

• Total Carbohydrate: 18g

• Dietary Fiber: 3g

• Sugars: 5g

• Protein: 25g

GRILLED CHICKEN CAESAR WRAPS

Prep Time: 15 minutes
Cooking Time: 10 minutes
Servings: 4
Ingredients:

- Four large flour tortillas
- 2 grilled chicken breasts, sliced thinly
- 2 cups romaine lettuce, chopped
- 1 cup cherry tomatoes, halved
- ½ cup Caesar dressing
- ½ cup grated Parmesan cheese
- Salt and pepper to taste

Directions:
1. **Prepare the Chicken:** Season the chicken breasts with salt and pepper. Grill until fully cooked, about 4-5 minutes per side. Let them rest for a few minutes, then slice thinly.
2. **Assemble the Wraps:** Lay out the tortillas. Divide the sliced chicken evenly among the tortillas, placing it in each centre.
3. **Add the Vegetables:** Top the chicken with chopped romaine lettuce and halved cherry tomatoes.
4. **Drizzle with Dressing:** Drizzle Caesar dressing evenly over the ingredients on each tortilla.
5. **Sprinkle with Parmesan:** Sprinkle grated cheese on top of each wrap.
6. **Wrap the Ingredients:** Fold in the sides of each tortilla, then roll tightly from the bottom up, enclosing the filling.
7. **Serve:** Slice each wrap in half diagonally and serve immediately.

Nutrition Facts (per Serving):

- Calories: 380
- Total Fat: 18g
- Saturated Fat: 5g
- Cholesterol: 70mg

- Sodium: 860mg
- Total Carbohydrates: 26g
- Dietary Fiber: 2g
- Sugars: 3g
- Protein: 28g

BBQ BACON RANCH BURGERS

Prep Time: 15 minutes
Cooking Time: 15 minutes
Servings: 4
Ingredients:

- 1 pound ground beef
- Four slices bacon, cooked crispy
- Four hamburger buns
- Four slices of cheddar cheese
- 1/4 cup barbecue sauce
- 1/4 cup ranch dressing
- Lettuce leaves
- Sliced tomatoes
- Sliced red onions
- Salt and pepper to taste

Directions:
1. Preheat your grill to medium-high heat.
2. season the ground beef with salt and pepper in a large mixing bowl. Divide the beef into four equal portions and shape them into burger patties.
3. Place the burger patties on the preheated grill and cook for 5-7 minutes on each side until they reach your desired level of doneness.
4. While cooking the burgers, toast the hamburger buns on the grill until lightly browned.
5. During the last couple minutes of cooking, place a slice of cheddar cheese on each burger patty and allow it to melt.
6. Remove the burgers from the grill and assemble them by placing each patty on a toasted bun.

7. Top each burger with a slice of crispy bacon, lettuce leaves, sliced tomatoes, and red onions.

8. In a small bowl, mix the barbecue sauce and ranch dressing. Drizzle this mixture over the assembled burgers.

9. Serve the BBQ Bacon Ranch Burgers immediately and enjoy!

Nutrition Facts (per Serving):

- **Calories:** 580 kcal
- **Total Fat:** 33g
  - Saturated Fat: 12g
  - Trans Fat: 1g
- **Cholesterol:** 110mg
- **Sodium:** 980mg
- **Total Carbohydrates:** 34g
  - Dietary Fiber: 2g
  - Sugars: 10g
- **Protein:** 36g

PHILLY CHEESESTEAK SANDWICHES

Prep Time: 15 minutes
Cooking Time: 20 minutes
Servings: 4
Ingredients:

- 1 lb ribeye steak, thinly sliced
- One onion, thinly sliced
- One green bell pepper, thinly sliced
- Four hoagie rolls sliced open
- 8 slices provolone cheese
- Two tablespoons of olive oil
- Salt and pepper to taste

Directions:

1. Heat olive oil in a large skillet over medium-high heat.

2. Add the sliced onions and green bell peppers to the skillet and sauté until they soften, about 5 minutes.

3. Push the vegetables to one side of the skillet and add the sliced ribeye steak to the other side. Cook, stirring occasionally, until the steak is browned and cooked through, about 5-7 minutes.

4. Mix the steak with the onions and peppers in the skillet once the steak is cooked. Season with salt and pepper to taste.

5. Preheat the oven to broil.

6. Open the hoagie rolls and place them on a baking sheet. Divide the steak mixture evenly among the rolls.

7. Top each sandwich with two slices of provolone cheese.

8. Place the baking sheet under the broiler and broil until the cheese is melted and bubbly, about 2-3 minutes.

9. Remove the sandwiches from the oven and serve hot.

Nutrition Facts (per Serving):

- Calories: 590
- Total Fat: 32g
- Saturated Fat: 14g
- Cholesterol: 105mg
- Sodium: 820mg
- Total Carbohydrate: 37g
- Dietary Fiber: 3g
- Sugars: 6g
- Protein: 38g

TERIYAKI CHICKEN SKEWERS

Prep Time: 20 minutes
Cooking Time: 10 minutes
Servings: 4
Ingredients:

- 1 lb (450g) boneless, skinless chicken breasts, cut into 1-inch cubes
- 1/4 cup soy sauce
- Two tablespoons honey
- Two tablespoons of rice vinegar
- One tablespoon of sesame oil
- Two cloves garlic, minced

- One teaspoon of grated ginger
- One tablespoon cornstarch
- 1/4 cup water
- Wooden skewers, soaked in water for 30 minutes
- Sesame seeds and chopped green onions for garnish (optional)

Directions:

1. In a small bowl, whisk together soy sauce, honey, rice vinegar, sesame oil, minced garlic, and grated ginger to make the teriyaki marinade.

2. Place the cubed chicken in a shallow dish or a resealable plastic bag. Pour half of the teriyaki marinade over the chicken and toss to coat. Cover (or seal) and refrigerate for at least 15 minutes or up to 2 hours.

3. Preheat your grill or grill pan over medium-high heat.

4. combine the remaining teriyaki marinade with cornstarch and water in a small saucepan. Cook over medium heat, stirring constantly, until the sauce thickens, about 2-3 minutes. Remove from heat and set aside.

5. Thread the marinated chicken onto the soaked wooden skewers.

6. Place the chicken skewers on the preheated grill and cook for 4-5 minutes per side until the chicken is cooked through and nicely charred on the edges.

7. Once cooked, remove the chicken skewers from the grill and place them on a serving platter.

8. Drizzle the thickened teriyaki sauce over the skewers and sprinkle with sesame seeds and chopped green onions, if desired.

9. Serve hot and enjoy!

Nutrition Facts (per Serving):

- Calories: 250
- Total Fat: 6g
- Saturated Fat: 1g
- Cholesterol: 85mg
- Sodium: 800mg
- Total Carbohydrate: 12g
- Dietary Fiber: 0.5g
- Sugars: 8g
- Protein: 35g

GRILLED VEGGIE PANINI

Prep Time: 15 minutes

 Cooking Time: 15 minutes

 Servings: 4

Ingredients:

- One medium zucchini, sliced lengthwise
- One medium eggplant, sliced lengthwise
- One red bell pepper, sliced
- One yellow bell pepper, sliced
- One red onion, sliced
- Four tablespoons of olive oil
- Salt and pepper to taste
- Eight slices of your favourite bread (sourdough or ciabatta work well)
- Eight slices of mozzarella cheese
- 1 cup baby spinach leaves
- Pesto sauce (optional)

Directions:

1. Preheat your grill or grill pan to medium-high heat.

2. In a large bowl, toss the sliced zucchini, eggplant, bell peppers, and onion with olive oil, salt, and pepper until evenly coated.

3. Grill the vegetables for 3-4 minutes per side until tender and lightly charred. Remove from heat and set aside.

4. Lay out the slices of bread. On each slice, layer a slice of mozzarella cheese, followed by a generous portion of grilled vegetables and a handful of spinach leaves.

5. If desired, spread pesto sauce on the remaining slices of bread before placing them on top of the vegetable and cheese layers.

6. Heat a panini press or grill pan over medium heat. Place the assembled sandwiches onto the panini press or grill pan and cook for 3-5 minutes until the bread is golden brown and the cheese is melted.

7. Once cooked, remove the sandwiches from the panini press or grill pan, slice in half, and serve hot.

Nutrition Facts (per Serving):

- Calories: 395 kcal
- Fat: 21g
- Carbohydrates: 39g

- Fiber: 6g
- Protein: 15g
- Sugar: 9g
- Sodium: 491mg

TURKEY CLUB SANDWICHES

Prep Time: 15 minutes
Cooking Time: 10 minutes
Servings: 4
Ingredients:

- 12 slices whole wheat bread
- 1/2 cup mayonnaise
- One tablespoon of Dijon mustard
- 1 pound thinly sliced roasted turkey breast
- Eight slices of cooked bacon
- Two tomatoes, thinly sliced
- 4 leaves iceberg lettuce
- Salt and pepper to taste

Directions:
1. **Prepare Ingredients:** Cook bacon until crispy, then drain on paper towels. Thinly slice tomatoes and wash lettuce leaves.
2. **Toast Bread:** Toast the slices of whole wheat bread until golden brown.
3. **Prepare Spread:** Mix mayonnaise and Dijon mustard in a small bowl until well combined.
4. **Assemble Sandwiches:** On four slices of toasted bread, spread a generous amount of the mayonnaise mixture.
5. **Layer Ingredients:** On each of the prepared slices of bread, layer the turkey, bacon, tomato slices, and lettuce leaves. Season with salt and pepper to taste.
6. **Top with Bread:** Place another slice of toasted bread on each sandwich.
7. **Secure Sandwiches:** Secure each sandwich with toothpicks to hold the layers together.
8. **Serve:** Cut each sandwich diagonally into halves and serve immediately.

Nutrition Facts (per Serving):
- **Calories:** 480 kcal

- **Total Fat:** 24g
  - Saturated Fat: 5g
  - Trans Fat: 0g
- **Cholesterol:** 70mg
- **Sodium:** 980mg
- **Total Carbohydrates:** 38g
  - Dietary Fiber: 6g
  - Sugars: 6g
- **Protein:** 28g

HAWAIIAN GRILLED CHICKEN BOWLS

Prep Time: 20 minutes
Cooking Time: 15 minutes
Servings: 4
Ingredients:

- Four boneless, skinless chicken breasts
- 2 cups pineapple chunks
- Two bell peppers, sliced (any colour you prefer)
- One red onion, sliced
- 1 cup cooked brown rice
- ½ cup teriyaki sauce
- Two tablespoons of olive oil
- Salt and pepper to taste
- Optional garnish: chopped cilantro, sesame seeds

Directions:
1. Preheat your grill to medium-high heat.
2. mix the teriyaki sauce with olive oil in a small bowl. Season with salt and pepper.
3. Place chicken breasts in a shallow dish and pour half of the teriyaki mixture over them. Allow to marinate for at least 10 minutes.
4. Thread pineapple chunks, bell peppers, and red onion onto skewers. Brush them with the remaining teriyaki mixture.
5. Grill chicken breasts on each side for 6-7 minutes or until fully cooked through with nice grill marks. At the same time, grill the skewers until the pineapple is caramelized and the vegetables are tender.

6. While the chicken grills, cook brown rice according to package instructions.
7. Once everything is cooked, slice the chicken breasts into strips.
8. To assemble the bowls, divide cooked rice among four bowls. Top each with grilled chicken strips, pineapple skewers, and sliced bell peppers and onions.
9. Garnish with chopped cilantro and sesame seeds if desired.
10. Serve immediately and enjoy your Hawaiian Grilled Chicken Bowls!

Nutrition Facts (per Serving):

- Calories: 380 kcal
- Total Fat: 10g
  - Saturated Fat: 1.5g
- Cholesterol: 90mg
- Sodium: 820mg
- Total Carbohydrate: 38g
  - Dietary Fiber: 4g
  - Sugars: 18g
- Protein: 35g

BLACK BEAN VEGGIE BURGERS

Prep Time: 15 minutes
Cooking Time: 10 minutes
Servings: 4
Ingredients:

- One can (15 ounces) black beans, drained and rinsed
- 1 cup cooked quinoa
- 1/2 cup breadcrumbs
- 1/4 cup finely chopped red onion
- 1/4 cup finely chopped bell pepper (any colour)
- Two cloves garlic, minced
- One teaspoon of ground cumin
- 1/2 teaspoon chilli powder
- Salt and pepper to taste
- One tablespoon of olive oil

Directions:

1. mash the black beans with a fork or potato masher until smooth in a large mixing bowl.

2. Add cooked quinoa, breadcrumbs, red onion, bell pepper, garlic, cumin, chilli powder, salt, and pepper to the mashed black beans. Mix until well combined.

3. Divide the mixture into four equal portions and shape each into a patty.

4. Heat olive oil in a skillet over medium heat.

5. carefully place the patties in the skillet once the oil is hot.

6. Cook the patties for about 4-5 minutes on each side until golden brown and heated through.

7. Remove the patties from the skillet and place them on a plate lined with paper towels to drain any excess oil.

8. Serve the black bean veggie burgers on buns with your favourite toppings and condiments.

Nutrition Facts (per Serving):

- Calories: 250
- Total Fat: 6g
- Saturated Fat: 1g
- Cholesterol: 0mg
- Sodium: 320mg
- Total Carbohydrate: 39g
- Dietary Fiber: 9g
- Sugars: 2g
- Protein: 11g

SHRIMP TACOS

Prep Time: 15 minutes
Cooking Time: 10 minutes
Servings: 4
Ingredients:

- 1 pound large shrimp, peeled and deveined
- One tablespoon of olive oil
- One teaspoon of chilli powder
- One teaspoon of garlic powder

- 1 teaspoon cumin
- Salt and pepper to taste
- Eight small corn tortillas
- 1 cup shredded lettuce
- 1 cup diced tomatoes
- 1/2 cup diced onions
- 1/4 cup chopped cilantro
- Lime wedges for serving
- **Optional toppings:** sliced avocado, sour cream, salsa

Directions:

1. toss the shrimp with olive oil, chilli powder, garlic powder, cumin, salt, and pepper until evenly coated.

2. Heat a skillet over medium-high heat. Add the seasoned shrimp and cook on each side for 2-3 minutes until they turn pink and opaque. Remove from heat and set aside.

3. In the same skillet, warm the corn tortillas for about 30 seconds on each side until they are soft and pliable. Remove from heat and keep warm.

4. To assemble the tacos, place some shredded lettuce on each tortilla, followed by cooked shrimp.

5. Top with diced tomatoes, onions, and chopped cilantro.

6. Serve the shrimp tacos with lime wedges on the side and any optional toppings you desire.

Nutrition Facts (per Serving):

- **Calories:** 275
- **Total Fat:** 7g
- **Saturated Fat:** 1g
- **Cholesterol:** 190mg
- **Sodium:** 410mg
- **Total Carbohydrates:** 27g
- **Dietary Fiber:** 5g
- **Sugars:** 3g
- **Protein:** 26g

CAPRESE PANINI

- **Prep Time:** 10 minutes
- **Cooking Time:** 5 minutes
- **Servings:** 2

Ingredients:

- One large ripe tomato, thinly sliced
- One ball of fresh mozzarella cheese, thinly sliced
- Four large fresh basil leaves
- Four slices of rustic Italian bread
- Two tablespoons of balsamic glaze
- 2 tablespoons olive oil
- Salt and pepper to taste

Directions:

1. Preheat your panini press or grill pan over medium heat.
2. Assemble the sandwiches: On two slices of bread, layer tomato slices, mozzarella slices, and basil leaves. Drizzle with balsamic glaze and season with salt and pepper. Top with the remaining slices of bread.
3. Brush the outside of the sandwiches with olive oil.
4. Place the sandwiches on the panini press or grill pan. If using a panini press, close the lid and cook for about 4-5 minutes or until the bread is golden brown and the cheese is melted. If using a grill pan, cook for 2-3 minutes on each side, pressing down with a spatula, until the bread is toasted and the cheese is melted.
5. Once done, remove the sandwiches from the heat and let them cool slightly before slicing them in half.
6. Serve immediately and enjoy your delicious Caprese Panini!

Nutrition Facts (per Serving):

- Calories: 380
- Total Fat: 18g
- Saturated Fat: 7g
- Cholesterol: 30mg
- Sodium: 480mg
- Total Carbohydrate: 39g

- Dietary Fiber: 3g
- Sugars: 9g
- Protein: 15g

BBQ PULLED PORK SANDWICHES

Prep Time: 15 minutes
Cooking Time: 8 hours
Servings: 6
Ingredients:

- 3 lbs pork shoulder or pork butt, trimmed of excess fat
- One onion, sliced
- Three cloves garlic, minced
- 1 cup barbecue sauce
- 1/4 cup brown sugar
- 1/4 cup apple cider vinegar
- One tablespoon of Worcestershire sauce
- One teaspoon of smoked paprika
- One teaspoon salt
- 1/2 teaspoon black pepper
- Six hamburger buns
- Coleslaw (optional for Serving)

Directions:
1. **Prep the Pork:** Place the sliced onion and minced garlic in the bottom of a slow cooker. Rub the pork shoulder with salt, pepper, and smoked paprika. Place the pork on the onions and garlic in the slow cooker.
2. **Make the Sauce:** In a bowl, mix the barbecue sauce, brown sugar, apple cider vinegar, and Worcestershire sauce. Pour the sauce over the pork shoulder.
3. **Slow Cook:** Cover the slow cooker and cook on low for 8 hours or until the pork is tender and easily shreds with a fork.
4. **Shred the Pork:** Once the pork is cooked, remove it from the slow cooker and shred it using two forks. Discard any excess fat.

5. **Finish the Sauce:** While shredding the pork, pour the cooking liquid from the slow cooker into a saucepan. Bring to a simmer over medium heat and let it reduce for about 10 minutes until slightly thickened.

6. **Combine and Serve:** Return the shredded pork to the slow cooker and pour the thickened sauce. Stir to combine.

7. **Assemble the Sandwiches:** Toast the hamburger buns if desired. Spoon a generous portion of the BBQ pulled pork onto the bottom half of each bun. Top with coleslaw if using, and cover with the top half of the bun.

8. Serve the BBQ pulled pork sandwiches immediately, with extra barbecue sauce on the side if desired.

Nutrition Facts (per Serving):

- Calories: 590
- Total Fat: 18g
- Saturated Fat: 6g
- Cholesterol: 150mg
- Sodium: 1160mg
- Total Carbohydrate: 54g
- Dietary Fiber: 2g
- Sugars: 25g
- Protein: 49g

CHICKEN FAJITA QUESADILLAS

Prep Time: 15 minutes
Cooking Time: 20 minutes
Servings: 4
Ingredients:

- Two boneless, skinless chicken breasts, thinly sliced
- One red bell pepper, thinly sliced
- One green bell pepper, thinly sliced
- One onion, thinly sliced
- 2 cups shredded cheddar cheese
- Four large flour tortillas
- 2 tablespoons olive oil

- Two teaspoons chilli powder
- One teaspoon cumin
- One teaspoon paprika
- Salt and pepper to taste
- Optional toppings: sour cream, salsa, guacamole

Directions:

1. heat one tablespoon of olive oil over medium-high heat in a large skillet. Add the sliced chicken breasts and cook until they are no longer pink in the centre, about 5-6 minutes. Remove from the skillet and set aside.
2. add the remaining tablespoon of olive oil in the same skillet. Add the sliced bell peppers and onion. Cook until they are tender-crisp, about 4-5 minutes. Season with chilli powder, cumin, paprika, salt, and pepper.
3. Return the cooked chicken to the skillet with the peppers and onions. Stir well to combine and cook for an additional 2-3 minutes.
4. Lay out one tortilla and sprinkle a portion of the shredded cheddar cheese evenly over half of the tortilla.
5. Spoon some of the chicken fajita mixture over the cheese.
6. Fold the tortilla half over the filling, creating a half-moon shape.
7. Repeat with the remaining tortillas and filling.
8. Heat a clean skillet over medium heat. Place a filled tortilla in the skillet and cook until the bottom is golden brown and crispy about 2-3 minutes.
9. Carefully flip the quesadilla and cook until the other side is golden brown and the cheese is melted, about 2-3 minutes more.
10. Remove from the skillet and let cool for a minute before slicing into wedges.
11. Serve hot with optional toppings like sour cream, salsa, or guacamole.

Nutrition Facts (per Serving):

- Calories: 475
- Total Fat: 23g
- Saturated Fat: 11g
- Cholesterol: 91mg
- Sodium: 665mg
- Total Carbohydrate: 29g
- Dietary Fiber: 3g
- Sugars: 3g

- Protein: 35g

GRILLED CHICKEN SALAD

Prep Time: 15 minutes
Cooking Time: 15 minutes
Servings: 4
Ingredients:

- Two boneless, skinless chicken breasts
- 6 cups mixed salad greens (such as lettuce, spinach, arugula)
- 1 cup cherry tomatoes, halved
- One cucumber, sliced
- One bell pepper, sliced
- 1/4 red onion, thinly sliced
- 1/2 cup crumbled feta cheese
- 1/4 cup sliced black olives
- 1/4 cup chopped fresh parsley
- Salt and black pepper to taste

For the Marinade:

- 3 tablespoons olive oil
- Two cloves garlic, minced
- One teaspoon dried oregano
- One teaspoon paprika
- Juice of 1 lemon
- Salt and black pepper to taste

For the Dressing:

- 1/4 cup olive oil
- Two tablespoons balsamic vinegar
- One teaspoon Dijon mustard
- One clove garlic, minced
- Salt and black pepper to taste

Directions:

1. **Marinate the Chicken:** In a bowl, whisk together the marinade ingredients. Place the chicken breasts in a shallow dish and pour the marinade over them. Cover and refrigerate for at least 30 minutes.
2. **Preheat the Grill:** Preheat your grill to medium-high heat.
3. **Grill the Chicken:** Remove the chicken from the marinade and discard any excess marinade. Grill the chicken breasts for 6-7 minutes per side until cooked through and no longer pink in the centre. Remove from the grill and let rest for a few minutes before slicing.
4. **Prepare the Salad:** In a large bowl, combine the salad greens, cherry tomatoes, cucumber, bell pepper, red onion, feta cheese, black olives, and chopped parsley. Toss to combine.
5. **Make the Dressing:** In a small bowl, whisk together the dressing ingredients until well combined.
6. **Assemble the Salad:** Slice the grilled chicken breasts and arrange them over the salad. Drizzle the dressing over the salad or serve it on the side.
7. Serve the grilled chicken salad immediately, garnished with additional parsley if desired.

Nutrition Facts (per Serving):
NOTE: NUTRITIONAL VALUES MAY VARY DEPENDING ON THE INGREDIENTS USED.

- Calories: 320
- Total Fat: 21g
  - Saturated Fat: 5g
  - Trans Fat: 0g
- Cholesterol: 80mg
- Sodium: 450mg
- Total Carbohydrate: 10g
  - Dietary Fiber: 3g
  - Sugars: 5g
- Protein: 25g

BUFFALO CHICKEN WRAPS

Prep Time: 15 minutes
Cooking Time: 15 minutes
Servings: 4
Ingredients:

- Two boneless, skinless chicken breasts
- 1/2 cup buffalo sauce
- Four large tortillas
- 1 cup shredded lettuce
- 1 cup diced tomatoes
- 1/2 cup crumbled blue cheese
- 1/4 cup ranch or blue cheese dressing
- Salt and pepper to taste
- One tablespoon olive oil

Directions:

1. Heat olive oil in a skillet over medium heat. Season chicken breasts with salt and pepper, then cook until browned and cooked through, about 6-8 minutes per side.
2. Remove chicken from the skillet and shred using two forks.
3. In a small saucepan, heat buffalo sauce until warm.
4. Toss shredded chicken in the warmed buffalo sauce until evenly coated.
5. Lay out tortillas on a flat surface. Divide the shredded lettuce, diced tomatoes, and crumbled blue cheese evenly among the tortillas.
6. Spoon the buffalo chicken mixture onto each tortilla.
7. Drizzle ranch or blue cheese dressing over the chicken.
8. Roll up the tortillas tightly, folding in the sides as you go, to create wraps.
9. Serve immediately, or wrap in foil and refrigerate for later.

Nutrition Facts (per Serving):

- Calories: 380
- Total Fat: 16g
- Saturated Fat: 5g
- Cholesterol: 70mg
- Sodium: 1250mg
- Total Carbohydrates: 29g
- Dietary Fiber: 2g
- Sugars: 2g
- Protein: 28g

MEDITERRANEAN GRILLED VEGGIE WRAPS

Prep Time: 15 minutes
Cooking Time: 15 minutes
Servings: 4
Ingredients:

- One medium eggplant, sliced lengthwise
- One medium zucchini, sliced lengthwise
- 1 medium yellow squash, sliced lengthwise
- 1 red bell pepper, sliced
- One yellow bell pepper, sliced
- One red onion, sliced
- Two tablespoons olive oil
- Salt and pepper to taste
- Four large whole wheat tortillas
- 1 cup hummus
- 1 cup crumbled feta cheese
- Fresh parsley leaves, for garnish (optional)

Directions:

1. Preheat your grill to medium-high heat.
2. In a large bowl, toss the sliced eggplant, zucchini, yellow squash, bell peppers, and onion with olive oil, salt, and pepper until evenly coated.
3. Place the vegetables on the preheated grill and cook for about 5-7 minutes per side until they are tender and have grill marks.
4. While the vegetables are grilling, warm the tortillas on the grill for 30 seconds per side.
5. Once the vegetables are grilled to your liking, remove them from the grill and set aside.
6. To assemble the wraps, spread about ¼ cup of hummus onto each tortilla, leaving a border around the edges.
7. Divide the grilled vegetables evenly among the tortillas, placing them on the hummus.
8. Sprinkle each wrap with crumbled feta cheese and garnish with fresh parsley leaves if desired.
9. Fold in the sides of each tortilla and then roll it up tightly.
10. Slice each wrap in half diagonally and serve immediately.

Nutrition Facts (per Serving):

- **Calories:** 380
- **Total Fat:** 18g
  - Saturated Fat: 5g
  - Trans Fat: 0g
- **Cholesterol:** 20mg
- **Sodium:** 710mg
- **Total Carbohydrate:** 45g
  - Dietary Fiber: 10g
  - Sugars: 7g
- **Protein:** 15g

TERIYAKI SALMON BOWLS

Prep Time: 15 minutes
Cooking Time: 15 minutes
Servings: 4
Ingredients:

- Four salmon fillets
- 1 cup of teriyaki sauce
- 2 cups of cooked rice
- 2 cups of mixed vegetables (such as broccoli, bell peppers, and carrots)
- Two tablespoons of olive oil
- Salt and pepper to taste
- Sesame seeds for garnish
- Sliced green onions for garnish

Directions:

1. **Marinate the Salmon:** Place the salmon fillets in a shallow dish and pour teriyaki sauce over them. Let them marinate for about 10 minutes while you prepare the other ingredients.
2. **Cook the Rice:** Prepare it according to package instructions and keep it warm.
3. **Prepare the Vegetables:** Heat olive oil in a large skillet over medium heat. Add the mixed vegetables and sauté for 5-7 minutes until tender but still crisp. Season with salt and pepper to taste.

4. **Cook the Salmon:** Heat a tablespoon of olive oil over medium-high heat in a separate skillet. Remove the salmon fillets from the marinade and place them in the skillet, skin side down. Cook for 3-4 minutes on each side until the salmon is cooked and flakes easily with a fork.

5. **Assemble the Bowls:** Divide the cooked rice among four bowls. Top each bowl with the sautéed vegetables and a cooked salmon fillet.

6. **Garnish:** Sprinkle sesame seeds and sliced green onions over the salmon bowls for garnish.

7. **Serve:** Serve the teriyaki salmon bowls immediately, and enjoy!

Nutrition Facts (per Serving):

- Calories: 450 kcal

- Fat: 15g

- Saturated Fat: 2.5g

- Cholesterol: 75mg

- Sodium: 1200mg

- Carbohydrates: 45g

- Fiber: 3g

- Sugars: 8g

- Protein: 35g

GRILLED CHEESE AND TOMATO SOUP

Prep Time: 10 minutes
Cooking Time: 25 minutes
Servings: 4
Ingredients:
For Grilled Cheese:

- Eight slices of bread (preferably sourdough)

- 2 cups shredded cheddar cheese

- Four tablespoons butter, softened

For Tomato Soup:

- One tablespoon olive oil

- One onion, finely chopped

- Two cloves garlic, minced

- One can (28 ounces) diced tomatoes

- 1 cup vegetable broth
- One teaspoon dried basil
- One teaspoon dried oregano
- Salt and pepper to taste
- 1/2 cup heavy cream (optional)

Directions:

1. **Prepare the Tomato Soup:**

· In a large pot, heat olive oil over medium heat. Add chopped onion and minced garlic. Cook until softened, about 5 minutes.

· Add diced tomatoes (with juices), vegetable broth, dried basil, and dried oregano to the pot. Season with salt and pepper. Bring to a simmer and cook for 15-20 minutes, stirring occasionally.

· Using an immersion blender or transferring in batches to a blender, blend the soup until smooth.

· If desired, stir in heavy cream for a creamier consistency. Adjust seasoning if necessary. Keep warm over low heat while preparing grilled cheese.

2. **Prepare the Grilled Cheese:**

· Heat a large skillet or griddle over medium heat.

· Spread softened butter on one side of each bread slice.

· Place four bread slices, buttered side down, on the skillet. Top each slice with shredded cheddar cheese. Place the remaining bread slices on top, buttered side up.

· Cook until the bottom is golden brown and the cheese is melting about 3-4 minutes. Flip and cook the other side until golden brown and the cheese completely melts.

· Remove from heat and let cool for a minute before cutting into halves or quarters.

3. **Serve:**

· Ladle the warm tomato soup into bowls.

· Serve grilled cheese alongside the soup for dipping or place on top.

· Enjoy your comforting grilled cheese and tomato soup!

Nutrition Facts (Per Serving): NUTRITIONAL VALUES MAY VARY DEPENDING ON SPECIFIC INGREDIENTS AND SERVING SIZE.

- Calories: Approximately 550 kcal
- Total Fat: 35g
  - Saturated Fat: 20g
- Cholesterol: 95mg

- Sodium: 1100mg
- Total Carbohydrates: 39g
  - Dietary Fiber: 4g
  - Sugars: 9g
- Protein: 20g

VEGGIE BURGER SLIDERS

Prep Time: 20 minutes
Cooking Time: 15 minutes
Servings: 4
Ingredients:

- One can (15 oz) black beans, drained and rinsed
- 1 cup cooked quinoa
- 1/2 cup breadcrumbs
- 1/4 cup finely chopped onion
- 1/4 cup grated carrots
- 1/4 cup chopped bell peppers (any colour)
- Two cloves garlic, minced
- One teaspoon ground cumin
- One teaspoon paprika
- Salt and pepper to taste
- Two tablespoons olive oil
- Eight slider buns
- Toppings of your choice (lettuce, tomato, avocado, etc.)

Directions:

1. mash the black beans with a fork or potato masher until smooth in a large bowl.
2. Add cooked quinoa, breadcrumbs, onion, carrots, bell peppers, garlic, cumin, paprika, salt, and pepper to the mashed beans. Mix well to combine all ingredients thoroughly.
3. Form the mixture into small patties about 2 inches in diameter.
4. Heat olive oil in a skillet over medium heat. Cook the patties on each side for about 3-4 minutes until golden brown and heated through.
5. While the patties cook, lightly toast the slider buns in the oven or skillet.

6. Assemble the sliders by placing each patty on a slider bun and topping with your favourite toppings.

7. Serve hot and enjoy!

Nutrition Facts (per Serving):

- Calories: 320 kcal
- Total Fat: 9g
  - Saturated Fat: 1g
  - Trans Fat: 0g
- Cholesterol: 0mg
- Sodium: 580mg
- Total Carbohydrate: 49g
  - Dietary Fiber: 10g
  - Sugars: 4g
- Protein: 11g

BBQ CHICKEN FLATBREADS

Prep Time: 15 minutes
Cooking Time: 15 minutes
Servings: 4
Ingredients:

- Four whole wheat flatbreads
- 2 cups cooked chicken breast, shredded
- 1 cup BBQ sauce
- 1 cup shredded mozzarella cheese
- One red onion, thinly sliced
- 1/2 cup chopped fresh cilantro
- Olive oil for brushing
- Salt and pepper to taste

Directions:

1. Preheat your oven to 400°F (200°C).
2. mix the shredded chicken with BBQ sauce until evenly coated in a bowl.
3. Place the flatbreads on a baking sheet. Brush each flatbread with olive oil.
4. Spread the BBQ chicken evenly over each flatbread.
5. Sprinkle shredded mozzarella cheese over the chicken.

6. Arrange sliced red onions on top.

7. Season with salt and pepper to taste.

8. Bake in the oven for 10-12 minutes until the cheese is melted and bubbly.

9. Once cooked, remove from the oven and sprinkle chopped cilantro over the flatbreads.

10. Slice the flatbreads and serve hot.

Nutrition Facts (per Serving):

- Calories: 420
- Total Fat: 11g
- Saturated Fat: 4g
- Cholesterol: 80mg
- Sodium: 1020mg
- Total Carbohydrate: 47g
- Dietary Fiber: 4g
- Sugars: 18g
- Protein: 34g

GREEK CHICKEN GYROS

Prep Time: 20 minutes

Cooking Time: 15 minutes

Servings: 4

Ingredients:

- Four boneless, skinless chicken breasts
- Four pita bread rounds
- 1 cup plain Greek yogurt
- Two tablespoons lemon juice
- Two cloves garlic, minced
- One teaspoon dried oregano
- One teaspoon dried thyme
- One teaspoon paprika
- Salt and pepper to taste
- One cucumber, thinly sliced

- One tomato, thinly sliced
- 1/2 red onion, thinly sliced
- 1/4 cup chopped fresh parsley
- Two tablespoons olive oil

Directions:

1. In a small bowl, mix Greek yoghurt, lemon juice, minced garlic, dried oregano, dried thyme, paprika, salt, and pepper. Set aside.
2. Slice the chicken breasts into thin strips and place them in a bowl. Pour half of the yoghurt mixture over the chicken and toss to coat evenly. Reserve the remaining yoghurt mixture for serving.
3. Heat olive oil in a large skillet over medium-high heat. Add the chicken strips and cook for 5-7 minutes until cooked and slightly browned.
4. While the chicken is cooking, warm the pita bread rounds in a separate skillet or oven.
5. spoon the reserved yoghurt mixture onto each pita bread round to assemble the gyros. Top with sliced cucumber, tomato, red onion, and chicken strips. Sprinkle with chopped parsley.
6. Fold the pita bread over the filling to form a gyro. Serve immediately.

DINNER RECIPES

GARLIC BUTTER STEAK BITES

Prep Time: 15 minutes
Cooking Time: 10 minutes
Servings: 4
Ingredients:

- 1 lb sirloin steak, cut into bite-sized pieces
- 3 tablespoons unsalted butter
- 4 cloves garlic, minced
- 1 teaspoon dried thyme
- 1 teaspoon dried rosemary
- Salt and pepper to taste
- Fresh parsley, chopped (for garnish)

Directions:

1. In a large skillet, melt 1 tablespoon of butter over medium-high heat.

2. Season the steak pieces with salt and pepper.

3. Once the skillet is hot, add the steak bites in a single layer. Cook for 2-3 minutes on each side or until browned and cooked to your desired level of doneness. Remove the steak from the skillet and set aside.

4. In the same skillet, melt the remaining butter over medium heat. Add minced garlic, dried thyme, and dried rosemary. Cook for 1-2 minutes, stirring constantly, until fragrant.

5. Return the cooked steak bites to the skillet. Toss them in the garlic butter mixture until well coated.

6. Remove from heat and transfer the steak bites to a serving platter.

7. Garnish with chopped parsley.

8. Serve hot and enjoy!

Nutrition Facts (per serving):

- Calories: 280
- Total Fat: 18g
- Saturated Fat: 9g
- Cholesterol: 90mg
- Sodium: 85mg
- Total Carbohydrates: 1g
- Dietary Fiber: 0g
- Sugars: 0g
- Protein: 27g

LEMON HERB GRILLED CHICKEN

- **Prep Time:** 10 minutes
- **Cooking Time:** 15 minutes
- **Servings:** 4

Ingredients:

- 4 boneless, skinless chicken breasts
- 2 lemons, juiced and zested
- 3 cloves garlic, minced

- 2 tablespoons fresh parsley, chopped
- 1 tablespoon fresh thyme leaves
- 1 tablespoon fresh rosemary, chopped
- 2 tablespoons olive oil
- Salt and pepper to taste

Directions:

1. Whisk together lemon juice, lemon zest, minced garlic, chopped parsley, thyme leaves, rosemary, olive oil, salt, and pepper in a small bowl.
2. Place chicken breasts in a shallow dish or resealable plastic bag and pour the marinade over them, ensuring all pieces are evenly coated. Marinate in the refrigerator for at least 30 minutes or up to 4 hours.
3. Preheat the grill to medium-high heat. Remove chicken from marinade and discard excess marinade.
4. Grill chicken breasts for 6-7 minutes per side, or until cooked through and juices run clear, with an internal temperature of 165°F (75°C).
5. Remove chicken from the grill and rest for a few minutes before serving.
6. Serve hot with your favourite side dishes.

Nutrition Facts (per serving):

- **Calories:** 250
- **Total Fat:** 10g
- **Saturated Fat:** 2g
- **Cholesterol:** 95mg
- **Sodium:** 350mg
- **Total Carbohydrate:** 5g
- **Dietary Fiber:** 1g
- **Sugars:** 1g
- **Protein:** 35g

SHRIMP SCAMPI LINGUINE

Prep Time: 15 minutes
Cooking Time: 15 minutes
Servings: 4
Ingredients:

- 1 pound linguine pasta
- 1 pound large shrimp, peeled and deveined
- 4 cloves garlic, minced
- 1/2 cup dry white wine
- 1/4 cup freshly squeezed lemon juice
- 1/4 cup extra virgin olive oil
- 1/4 cup chopped fresh parsley
- Salt and black pepper to taste
- Crushed red pepper flakes (optional)
- Grated Parmesan cheese for serving

Directions:

1. Cook linguine according to package instructions until al dente. Drain and set aside.
2. In a large skillet, heat olive oil over medium heat. Add minced garlic and cook until fragrant, about 1 minute.
3. Increase the heat to medium-high and add the shrimp to the skillet. Season with salt, black pepper, and red pepper flakes if using. Cook the shrimp until pink and cooked through, about 2-3 minutes per side. Remove the shrimp from the skillet and set aside.
4. Deglaze the skillet with white wine, scraping up any browned bits from the bottom of the pan. Allow the wine to reduce by half, about 2-3 minutes.
5. Add lemon juice to the skillet and stir to combine with the wine.
6. Return the cooked shrimp to the skillet, along with the cooked linguine and chopped parsley. Toss everything together until well combined and heated through.
7. Taste and adjust seasoning if needed.
8. Serve hot, garnished with grated Parmesan cheese.

Nutrition Facts (per serving):

- Calories: 520
- Total Fat: 15g
- Saturated Fat: 2g
- Cholesterol: 180mg

- Sodium: 330mg
- Total Carbohydrate: 62g
- Dietary Fiber: 3g
- Sugars: 2g
- Protein: 30g

BBQ RIBS

Prep Time: 15 minutes
Cooking Time: 2 hours
Servings: 4
Ingredients:

- 2 racks of pork baby back ribs
- 1 cup BBQ sauce (your favourite brand or homemade)
- 2 tablespoons brown sugar
- 1 tablespoon paprika
- 1 tablespoon garlic powder
- 1 tablespoon onion powder
- Salt and pepper to taste

Directions:

1. Preheat your grill to medium heat (around 300°F or 150°C).
2. Prepare the ribs by removing the membrane from the back of the racks. You can do this by loosening a corner with a knife or your fingers and pulling it off.
3. Mix the brown sugar, paprika, garlic powder, onion powder, salt, and pepper in a small bowl to create a rub.
4. Rub the spice mixture generously over both sides of the ribs.
5. Place the ribs on the grill, bone side down, and cook for about 1 hour, turning occasionally to ensure even cooking.
6. After the first hour, baste the ribs with BBQ sauce, using a brush to coat them evenly. Continue cooking for another hour, basting with more sauce every 15 minutes.

7. Check for doneness by inserting a meat thermometer into the thickest part of the ribs. They should reach an internal temperature of at least 145°F (63°C) for medium-rare or 160°F (71°C) for medium.

8. Once done, remove the ribs from the grill and let them rest for a few minutes before slicing and serving.

Nutrition Facts (per serving):

- Calories: 550
- Total Fat: 35g
- Saturated Fat: 12g
- Cholesterol: 150mg
- Sodium: 800mg
- Total Carbohydrates: 22g
- Dietary Fiber: 1g
- Sugars: 18g
- Protein: 35g

TERIYAKI BEEF STIR-FRY

Prep Time: 15 minutes
Cooking Time: 15 minutes
Servings: 4
Ingredients:

- 1 lb (450g) beef sirloin, thinly sliced
- 1 cup broccoli florets
- 1 red bell pepper, sliced
- 1 yellow bell pepper, sliced
- 1 onion, sliced
- 2 cloves garlic, minced
- 1 tablespoon vegetable oil
- ½ cup teriyaki sauce
- 2 tablespoons soy sauce
- 2 tablespoons honey
- 1 tablespoon cornstarch

- 2 tablespoons water
- Sesame seeds and green onions for garnish
- Cooked rice or noodles for serving

Directions:

1. Mix teriyaki sauce, soy sauce, and honey in a small bowl. Set aside.
2. In another bowl, dissolve cornstarch in water. Set aside.
3. Heat vegetable oil in a large skillet or wok over medium-high heat.
4. Add sliced beef and minced garlic to the skillet. Stir-fry until the beef is browned and cooked through, about 3-4 minutes. Remove the beef from the skillet and set aside.
5. In the same skillet, add a bit more oil if needed. Stir-fry the broccoli, bell peppers, and onion until tender-crisp, about 4-5 minutes.
6. Return the beef to the skillet with the vegetables.
7. Pour the teriyaki sauce mixture over the beef and vegetables. Stir well to combine.
8. Add the dissolved cornstarch to the skillet, stirring constantly until the sauce thickens, about 1-2 minutes.
9. Remove from heat and garnish with sesame seeds and chopped green onions.
10. Serve the teriyaki beef stir-fry hot cooked rice or noodles.

Nutrition Facts (per serving):

- Calories: 345
- Total Fat: 14g
- Saturated Fat: 4g
- Cholesterol: 71mg
- Sodium: 1143mg
- Total Carbohydrate: 25g
- Dietary Fiber: 3g
- Sugars: 15g
- Protein: 30g

GRILLED SALMON WITH DILL SAUCE

Prep Time: 10 minutes

Cooking Time: 10 minutes

Servings: 4

Ingredients:

- 4 salmon fillets (about 6 ounces each)
- Salt and pepper to taste
- 2 tablespoons olive oil
- 1/4 cup chopped fresh dill
- 2 tablespoons lemon juice
- 1/2 cup plain Greek yogurt
- 2 cloves garlic, minced
- 1 tablespoon Dijon mustard
- 1 teaspoon honey

Directions:

1. Preheat your grill to medium-high heat.
2. Season the salmon fillets with salt, pepper, and olive oil.
3. Mix the chopped dill, lemon juice, Greek yoghurt, minced garlic, Dijon mustard, and honey in a small bowl to make the dill sauce. Set aside.
4. Place the salmon fillets on the grill, skin-side down, and cook for 4-5 minutes on each side or until desired doneness. You can also use a grill basket or aluminium foil to prevent salmon from sticking to the grill.
5. Once the salmon is cooked through, remove from the grill and transfer to a serving platter.
6. Serve the grilled salmon hot with a generous dollop of the prepared dill sauce on top.

Nutrition Facts (per serving):

- **Calories:** 320
- **Total Fat:** 18g
- **Saturated Fat:** 3.5g
- **Cholesterol:** 85mg
- **Sodium:** 170mg
- **Total Carbohydrate:** 3g

- **Dietary Fiber:** 0g
- **Sugars:** 2g
- **Protein:** 34g

BBQ CHICKEN PIZZA

Prep Time: 15 minutes
Cooking Time: 15 minutes
Servings: 4
Ingredients:

- 1 pre-made pizza dough or homemade dough
- 1 cup cooked chicken breast, shredded or diced
- 1/2 cup barbecue sauce
- 1 cup shredded mozzarella cheese
- 1/4 red onion, thinly sliced
- 1/4 cup fresh cilantro leaves, chopped
- Salt and pepper to taste
- Olive oil for brushing

Directions:

1. Preheat your oven to 425°F (220°C).
2. Roll the pizza dough onto a lightly floured surface to your desired thickness.
3. Transfer the dough to a lightly greased baking sheet or pizza stone.
4. Brush the surface of the dough lightly with olive oil.
5. Spread barbecue sauce evenly over the dough, leaving a small border around the edges.
6. Sprinkle shredded chicken evenly over the sauce.
7. Top with sliced red onion and shredded mozzarella cheese.
8. Season with salt and pepper to taste.
9. Bake in the oven for 12-15 minutes until the crust is golden brown and the cheese is melted and bubbly.
10. Remove from the oven and sprinkle chopped cilantro over the hot pizza.

11.   Let it cool for a few minutes before slicing.

12.   Serve hot and enjoy your delicious BBQ Chicken Pizza!

Nutrition Facts (per serving):

- Calories: 380
- Total Fat: 12g
  - Saturated Fat: 4.5g
  - Trans Fat: 0g
- Cholesterol: 45mg
- Sodium: 880mg
- Total Carbohydrate: 45g
  - Dietary Fiber: 2g
  - Sugars: 14g
- Protein: 23g

Honey Mustard Pork Chops
Prep Time: 10 minutes
Cooking Time: 20 minutes
Servings: 4
Ingredients:

- 4 pork chops (about 1 inch thick)
- 1/4 cup Dijon mustard
- 1/4 cup honey
- 2 cloves garlic, minced
- 2 tablespoons olive oil
- Salt and pepper to taste
- Fresh parsley for garnish (optional)

Directions:

1. Preheat your oven to 375°F (190°C).

2. Whisk together Dijon mustard, honey, minced garlic, olive oil, salt, and pepper in a small bowl.

3. Place the pork chops in a shallow dish or resealable plastic bag, and pour the honey mustard mixture over them. Ensure the chops are evenly coated. Let marinate for at least 10 minutes or overnight in the refrigerator for deeper flavour.

4. Heat a skillet over medium-high heat. Once hot, add a drizzle of olive oil.

5. Remove the pork chops from the marinade, allowing excess to drip off, and place them in the skillet.

6. Sear the pork chops on each side for 2-3 minutes until golden brown.

7. Transfer the skillet to the preheated oven and bake for 12-15 minutes, or until the pork's internal temperature reaches 145°F (63°C).

8. Remove from the oven and let the pork chops rest for a few minutes before serving.

9. Garnish with fresh parsley if desired. Serve hot with your favourite sides.

Nutrition Facts (per serving):

- Calories: 320
- Total Fat: 14g
- Saturated Fat: 3g
- Cholesterol: 90mg
- Sodium: 330mg
- Total Carbohydrate: 14g
- Dietary Fiber: 0.5g
- Sugars: 12g
- Protein: 32g

CAJUN SHRIMP AND SAUSAGE SKEWERS

Prep Time: 20 minutes
Cooking Time: 10 minutes
Servings: 4
Ingredients:

- 1 lb large shrimp, peeled and deveined
- 1 lb smoked sausage, cut into chunks
- 2 bell peppers, cut into chunks
- 1 red onion, cut into chunks
- 2 tablespoons olive oil
- 2 tablespoons Cajun seasoning

- Salt and pepper to taste
- Wooden skewers, soaked in water for 30 minutes

Directions:

1. Preheat the grill to medium-high heat.
2. Toss shrimp, sausage, bell peppers, onion with olive oil, Cajun seasoning, salt, and pepper until evenly coated in a large bowl.
3. Thread shrimp, sausage, peppers, and onion onto skewers, alternating ingredients.
4. Place skewers on the preheated grill and cook for 3-4 minutes per side, or until shrimp is pink sau, sage is heated through, and vegetables are tender and slightly charred.
5. Remove skewers from the grill and serve hot.

Nutrition Facts: SERVING SIZE: 1 SKEWER

- Calories: 320
- Total Fat: 20g
  - Saturated Fat: 6g
  - Trans Fat: 0g
- Cholesterol: 200mg
- Sodium: 1200mg
- Total Carbohydrates: 10g
  - Dietary Fiber: 2g
  - Sugars: 4g
- Protein: 25g

TERIYAKI BEEF KABOBS

Prep Time: 20 minutes
Cooking Time: 10 minutes
Servings: 4
Ingredients:

- 1 lb (450g) beef sirloin, cut into 1-inch cubes
- 1/2 cup teriyaki sauce
- 2 tablespoons soy sauce
- 2 tablespoons honey

- 2 cloves garlic, minced
- 1 teaspoon grated fresh ginger
- 1 bell pepper, cut into chunks
- 1 red onion, cut into chunks
- 8-10 cherry tomatoes
- Wooden skewers, soaked in water for 30 minutes

Directions:

1. Mix teriyaki sauce, soy sauce, honey, minced garlic, and grated ginger in a bowl. Add the beef cubes to the marinade and let it marinate for at least 15 minutes or up to 2 hours in the refrigerator.
2. Preheat your grill to medium-high heat.
3. Thread marinated beef cubes, bell pepper chunks, onion chunks, and cherry tomatoes onto the soaked wooden skewers, alternating ingredients.
4. Place the kabobs on the preheated grill and cook for about 8-10 minutes, turning occasionally, until the beef is cooked to your desired level of doneness and the vegetables are tender and slightly charred.
5. Remove the kabobs from the grill and let them rest for a few minutes before serving.
6. Serve the teriyaki beef kabobs hot with steamed rice or grilled vegetables.

Nutrition Facts (per serving):

- **Calories:** 280
- **Total Fat:** 12g
- **Saturated Fat:** 4g
- **Cholesterol:** 70mg
- **Sodium:** 980mg
- **Total Carbohydrate:** 15g
- **Dietary Fiber:** 2g
- **Sugars:** 10g
- **Protein:** 26g

GRILLED VEGETABLE STIR-FRY

Prep Time: 15 minutes
Cooking Time: 15 minutes
Servings: 4
Ingredients:

- 2 zucchinis, sliced
- 1 red bell pepper, sliced
- 1 yellow bell pepper, sliced
- 1 red onion, sliced
- 1 cup broccoli florets
- 1 cup snap peas
- 3 tablespoons olive oil
- 3 cloves garlic, minced
- Salt and pepper to taste
- 2 tablespoons soy sauce
- 1 tablespoon sesame oil
- 1 tablespoon honey
- 1 teaspoon grated ginger
- Sesame seeds for garnish
- Cooked rice or noodles for serving

Directions:

1. Preheat your grill to medium-high heat.
2. In a large bowl, toss the sliced zucchini, red bell pepper, yellow bell pepper, red onion, broccoli florets, and snap peas with 2 tablespoons of olive oil, minced garlic, salt, and pepper.
3. Grill the vegetables in batches until they are tender and slightly charred, about 5-7 minutes per batch. Remove from the grill and set aside.
4. Whisk the remaining olive oil, soy sauce, sesame oil, honey, and grated ginger in a small bowl to make the stir-fry sauce.
5. Heat a large skillet or wok over medium-high heat. Add the grilled vegetables to the skillet and pour the stir-fry sauce.
6. Cook, stirring constantly, for 2-3 minutes until the vegetables are heated through and coated in the sauce.

7. Serve the grilled vegetable stir-fry over cooked rice or noodles garnished with sesame seeds.

Nutrition Facts (per serving):

- Calories: 210 kcal
- Total Fat: 11g
    - Saturated Fat: 1.5g
    - Trans Fat: 0g
- Cholesterol: 0mg
- Sodium: 480mg
- Total Carbohydrate: 25g
    - Dietary Fiber: 5g
    - Sugars: 12g
- Protein: 5g
- Vitamin D: 0%
- Calcium: 6%
- Iron: 8%
- Potassium: 15%

CHIMICHURRI STEAK

Prep Time: 15 minutes
Cooking Time: 10 minutes
Servings: 4
Ingredients:

- 4 sirloin steaks (about 6-8 ounces each)
- Salt and pepper to taste
- For Chimichurri Sauce:
    - 1 cup fresh parsley, chopped
    - 4 cloves garlic, minced
    - 1/4 cup red wine vinegar
    - 1/2 cup extra virgin olive oil
    - 1 tablespoon dried oregano
    - 1 teaspoon red pepper flakes (adjust to taste)
    - Salt and pepper to taste
- For serving:

- Grilled vegetables
- Mashed potatoes or rice

Directions:

1. **Prepare the Chimichurri Sauce:** In a small bowl, combine chopped parsley, minced garlic, red wine vinegar, olive oil, dried oregano, red pepper flakes, salt, and pepper. Mix well and set aside.

2. **Preheat Grill:** Preheat your grill to medium-high heat.

3. **Season Steaks:** Season the sirloin steaks generously with salt and pepper on both sides.

4. **Grill Steaks:** Place the steaks on the preheated grill and cook for 4-5 minutes on each side for medium-rare, or adjust the cooking time according to desired doneness.

5. **Rest Steaks:** Once cooked to your liking, remove the steaks from the grill and let them rest for about 5 minutes.

6. **Serve:** Slice the steaks against the grain and drizzle with the prepared chimichurri sauce. Serve with grilled vegetables and mashed potatoes or rice.

Nutrition Facts (per serving):

- Calories: 450
- Total Fat: 32g
- Saturated Fat: 8g
- Cholesterol: 90mg
- Sodium: 180mg
- Total Carbohydrates: 2g
- Dietary Fiber: 1g
- Sugars: 0g
- Protein: 38g

GARLIC BUTTER SHRIMP PASTA

Prep Time: 10 minutes
Cooking Time: 15 minutes
Servings: 4
Ingredients:

- 12 ounces of linguine pasta

- 1 pound of large shrimp, peeled and deveined
- 4 tablespoons of unsalted butter
- 4 cloves of garlic, minced
- 1/4 teaspoon of red pepper flakes (optional)
- Salt and black pepper to taste
- 1/4 cup of freshly chopped parsley
- 1/4 cup of grated Parmesan cheese
- Lemon wedges for serving

Directions:

1. Cook the linguine pasta according to package instructions until al dente. Drain and set aside, reserving 1/2 cup of pasta water.
2. Melt the butter in a large skillet over medium heat. Add the minced garlic and red pepper flakes if using. Sauté for 1-2 minutes until fragrant.
3. Add the shrimp to the skillet and season with salt and black pepper. Cook for 2-3 minutes on each side until they turn pink and opaque.
4. Add the cooked pasta to the skillet along with the chopped parsley. Toss well to combine, adding reserved pasta water if needed to loosen the sauce.
5. Sprinkle grated Parmesan cheese over the pasta and toss again until the cheese is melted and everything is well coated.
6. Taste and adjust seasoning if necessary.
7. Serve the garlic butter shrimp pasta hot with lemon wedges on the side for squeezing.

Nutrition Facts (per serving):

- Calories: 425
- Total Fat: 14g
  - Saturated Fat: 8g
- Cholesterol: 250mg
- Sodium: 385mg
- Total Carbohydrates: 46g
  - Dietary Fiber: 2g
  - Sugars: 2g

- Protein: 30g

HAWAIIAN BBQ CHICKEN BOWLS

Prep Time: 15 minutes
Cooking Time: 25 minutes
Servings: 4
Ingredients:
For the Chicken:

- 4 boneless, skinless chicken breasts
- 1 cup pineapple juice
- ½ cup BBQ sauce
- 2 cloves garlic, minced
- Salt and pepper to taste

For the Rice:

- 2 cups cooked rice (white or brown)
- 1 tablespoon soy sauce
- 1 tablespoon sesame oil

For the Bowl Assembly:

- 2 cups chopped fresh pineapple
- 1 red bell pepper, sliced
- 1 green bell pepper, sliced
- 1 red onion, sliced
- 1 tablespoon olive oil
- Salt and pepper to taste
- ¼ cup chopped green onions (for garnish)
- Sesame seeds (for garnish)

Directions:

1. **Marinate the Chicken:** In a bowl, mix pineapple juice, BBQ sauce, minced garlic, salt, and pepper. Place chicken breasts in a resealable plastic bag or shallow dish and pour the marinade over them. Marinate in the refrigerator for at least 30 minutes.

2. **Cook the Rice:** Prepare rice according to package instructions. Once cooked, fluff the rice with a fork and mix in soy sauce and sesame oil. Keep warm.

3. **Preheat the Grill or Grill Pan:** Preheat your grill or pan over medium-high heat.

4. **Grill the Chicken:** Remove the chicken from the marinade and discard the excess marinade. Grill the chicken for about 6-7 minutes per side, or until cooked through and no longer pink in the center. Remove from heat and let it rest for a few minutes before slicing.

5. **Prepare the Pineapple and Vegetables:** In a bowl, toss chopped pineapple, sliced bell peppers, and red onion with olive oil, salt, and pepper.

6. **Grill the Pineapple and Vegetables:** Grill the pineapple and vegetables until they are slightly charred and tender, about 5-7 minutes.

7. **Assemble the Bowls:** Divide rice among serving bowls. Top with sliced grilled chicken, grilled pineapple, and vegetables.

8. **Garnish:** Garnish with chopped green onions and sesame seeds.

Nutrition Facts (per serving):

- Calories: 450
- Total Fat: 9g
- Saturated Fat: 1.5g
- Cholesterol: 90mg
- Sodium: 550mg
- Total Carbohydrate: 54g
- Dietary Fiber: 5g
- Sugars: 23g
- Protein: 38g

LEMON PEPPER GRILLED TILAPIA

Prep Time: 10 minutes
Cooking Time: 10 minutes
Servings: 4
Ingredients:

- 4 tilapia fillets

- 2 tablespoons olive oil
- 2 tablespoons lemon juice
- 2 teaspoons lemon zest
- 1 teaspoon black pepper
- 1 teaspoon garlic powder
- 1 teaspoon paprika
- Salt to taste
- Lemon wedges for serving
- Chopped fresh parsley for garnish

Directions:

1. Preheat your grill to medium-high heat.
2. Whisk together olive oil, lemon juice, lemon zest, black pepper, garlic powder, paprika, and salt in a small bowl.
3. Pat the tilapia fillets dry with paper towels and place them on a plate.
4. Brush both sides of each fillet with the lemon-pepper mixture, ensuring they are evenly coated.
5. Place the fillets on the preheated grill and cook on each side for 4-5 minutes or until the fish is opaque and easily flakes with a fork.
6. Once cooked, remove the tilapia from the grill and transfer to a serving platter.
7. Garnish with chopped parsley and serve with lemon wedges on the side.

Nutrition Facts (per serving):

- Calories: 190
- Total Fat: 9g
- Saturated Fat: 1.5g
- Cholesterol: 85mg
- Sodium: 100mg
- Total Carbohydrate: 1g
- Dietary Fiber: 0g
- Sugars: 0g
- Protein: 25g

STEAK AND MUSHROOM SKEWERS

Prep Time: 20 minutes
Cooking Time: 10 minutes
Servings: 4
Ingredients:

- 1 lb (450g) sirloin steak, cut into 1-inch cubes
- 1 lb (450g) button mushrooms, cleaned
- 1 red bell pepper, cut into chunks
- 1 red onion, cut into chunks
- 2 tablespoons olive oil
- 2 cloves garlic, minced
- 2 tablespoons soy sauce
- 1 tablespoon Worcestershire sauce
- 1 teaspoon Dijon mustard
- Salt and black pepper to taste
- Wooden or metal skewers

Directions:

1. Mix olive oil, minced garlic, soy sauce, Worcestershire sauce, Dijon mustard, salt, and black pepper in a small bowl.

2. Place the steak cubes in a large resealable plastic bag and pour the marinade over them. Seal the bag and shake until the steak is well coated. Marinate in the refrigerator for at least 1 hour, or overnight for best results.

3. Preheat your grill or grill pan to medium-high heat.

4. Thread the marinated steak cubes onto skewers, alternating with mushrooms, bell pepper, and onion.

5. Brush the skewers with any remaining marinade.

6. Grill the skewers for about 3-4 minutes per side or until the steak reaches your desired level of doneness and the vegetables are tender.

7. Remove the skewers from the grill and let them rest for a few minutes before serving.

8. Serve the steak and mushroom skewers hot with your favourite side dishes.

Nutrition Facts (per serving):

- Calories: 320
- Total Fat: 16g
- Saturated Fat: 4g
- Cholesterol: 80mg
- Sodium: 630mg
- Total Carbohydrate: 9g
- Dietary Fiber: 2g
- Sugars: 4g
- Protein: 35g

SPICY GRILLED SHRIMP TACOS

Prep Time: 20 minutes
Cooking Time: 10 minutes
Servings: 4
Ingredients:

- 1 lb (450g) sirloin steak, cut into 1-inch cubes
- 1 lb (450g) button mushrooms, cleaned
- 1 red bell pepper, cut into chunks
- 1 red onion, cut into chunks
- 2 tablespoons olive oil
- 2 cloves garlic, minced
- 2 tablespoons soy sauce
- 1 tablespoon Worcestershire sauce
- 1 teaspoon Dijon mustard
- Salt and black pepper to taste
- Wooden or metal skewers

Directions:

1. Mix olive oil, minced garlic, soy sauce, Worcestershire sauce, Dijon mustard, salt, and black pepper in a small bowl.
2. Place the steak cubes in a large resealable plastic bag and pour the marinade over them. Seal the bag and shake until the steak is well

coated. Marinate in the refrigerator for at least 1 hour, or overnight for best results.

3. Preheat your grill or grill pan to medium-high heat.

4. Thread the marinated steak cubes onto skewers, alternating with mushrooms, bell pepper, and onion.

5. Brush the skewers with any remaining marinade.

6. Grill the skewers for about 3-4 minutes per side or until the steak reaches your desired level of doneness and the vegetables are tender.

7. Remove the skewers from the grill and let them rest for a few minutes before serving.

8. Serve the steak and mushroom skewers hot with your favourite side dishes.

Nutrition Facts (per serving):

- Calories: 320
- Total Fat: 16g
- Saturated Fat: 4g
- Cholesterol: 80mg
- Sodium: 630mg
- Total Carbohydrate: 9g
- Dietary Fiber: 2g
- Sugars: 4g
- Protein: 35g

GRILLED VEGGIE PASTA PRIMAVERA

Prep Time: 15 minutes
Cooking Time: 20 minutes
Servings: 4
Ingredients:

- 8 ounces of your preferred pasta (spaghetti, penne, or fusilli)
- 2 cups of mixed vegetables (such as bell peppers, zucchini, mushrooms, and cherry tomatoes), sliced
- 2 tablespoons olive oil
- Salt and black pepper to taste

- 2 cloves garlic, minced
- 1/4 cup grated Parmesan cheese
- 1 tablespoon fresh basil, chopped (optional)
- Lemon wedges for serving

Directions:

1. **Preheat** your grill to medium-high heat.
2. **Cook** the pasta according to package instructions until al dente. Drain and set aside.
3. **Toss** the mixed vegetables with olive oil, salt, and black pepper in a large bowl until evenly coated.
4. **Grill** the vegetables for about 5-7 minutes, turning occasionally until tender and lightly charred. Remove from the grill and set aside.
5. **Heat** a tablespoon of olive oil over medium heat in a large skillet. Add the minced garlic and sauté for about 1 minute until fragrant.
6. **Add** the grilled vegetables to the skillet and toss to combine with the garlic.
7. **Add** the cooked pasta to the skillet and toss everything together until heated.
8. **Remove** from heat and sprinkle with grated Parmesan cheese and chopped basil if using.
9. **Serve** immediately with lemon wedges on the side for squeezing over the pasta.

Nutrition Facts (per serving):

- **Calories:** 320
- **Total Fat:** 10g
- **Saturated Fat:** 2g
- **Cholesterol:** 5mg
- **Sodium:** 180mg
- **Total Carbohydrates:** 50g
- **Dietary Fiber:** 5g
- **Sugars:** 4g
- **Protein:** 10g

BOURBON GLAZED PORK TENDERLOIN

Prep Time: 15 minutes
Cooking Time: 25 minutes
Servings: 4
Ingredients:

- 2 pork tenderloins (about 1 pound each)
- Salt and pepper to taste
- 1 tablespoon olive oil
- 1/4 cup bourbon
- 1/4 cup brown sugar
- 2 tablespoons Dijon mustard
- 2 cloves garlic, minced
- 1 teaspoon Worcestershire sauce
- 1/4 teaspoon red pepper flakes (optional)
- Fresh parsley, chopped (for garnish)

Directions:

1. Preheat your oven to 375°F (190°C).
2. Season the pork tenderloins generously with salt and pepper.
3. In a large ovenproof skillet, heat olive oil over medium-high heat. Add the pork tenderloins and sear them on all sides until browned, about 2-3 minutes per side.
4. Mix bourbon, brown sugar, Dijon mustard, minced garlic, Worcestershire sauce, and red pepper flakes in a small bowl.
5. Pour the bourbon glaze over the pork tenderloins in the skillet, turning them to coat evenly.
6. Transfer the skillet to the preheated oven and roast for about 20-25 minutes or until the internal temperature of the pork reaches 145°F (63°C), basting occasionally with the glaze.
7. Once cooked, remove the skillet from the oven and transfer the pork tenderloins to a cutting board. Tent them loosely with foil and let them rest for 5-10 minutes.
8. Slice the pork tenderloins into medallions and drizzle with any remaining glaze from the skillet.

9. Garnish with chopped parsley before serving.

Nutrition Facts (per serving):

- Calories: 320
- Total Fat: 10g
- Saturated Fat: 2.5g
- Cholesterol: 100mg
- Sodium: 280mg
- Total Carbohydrate: 11g
- Dietary Fiber: 0.5g
- Sugars: 9g
- Protein: 40g

MEDITERRANEAN GRILLED CHICKEN

Prep Time: 15 minutes
Cooking Time: 15 minutes
Servings: 4
Ingredients:

- 4 boneless, skinless chicken breasts
- 1/4 cup olive oil
- 3 cloves garlic, minced
- 1 teaspoon dried oregano
- 1 teaspoon dried basil
- 1/2 teaspoon dried thyme
- 1/2 teaspoon dried rosemary
- Salt and black pepper to taste
- Juice of 1 lemon
- 1 tablespoon balsamic vinegar
- 1/4 cup chopped fresh parsley (for garnish)
- Lemon wedges (for serving)

Directions:

1. Whisk together olive oil, minced garlic, dried oregano, basil, thyme, rosemary, salt, pepper, lemon juice, and balsamic vinegar in a bowl.

2. Place the chicken breasts in a resealable plastic bag or shallow dish and pour the marinade over them. Seal the bag or cover the dish, then marinate in the refrigerator for at least 30 minutes or up to 4 hours, turning occasionally to ensure even coating.

3. Preheat the grill to medium-high heat.

4. Remove the chicken from the marinade and discard any excess marinade. Place the chicken breasts on the preheated grill and cook for 6-7 minutes per side until the internal temperature reaches 165°F (75°C) and the chicken is no longer pink in the centre.

5. Once cooked, remove the chicken from the grill and let it rest for a few minutes.

6. Garnish with chopped parsley and serve with lemon wedges on the side.

Nutrition Facts (per serving):

- Calories: 280
- Total Fat: 14g
    - Saturated Fat: 2g
    - Trans Fat: 0g
- Cholesterol: 90mg
- Sodium: 350mg
- Total Carbohydrate: 2g
    - Dietary Fiber: 1g
    - Sugars: 0g
- Protein: 34g

GRILLED SHRIMP COCKTAIL

Prep Time: 15 minutes
Cooking Time: 5 minutes
Servings: 4
Ingredients:

- 1 pound large shrimp, peeled and deveined
- 2 tablespoons olive oil
- Salt and pepper to taste
- 1 lemon, cut into wedges
- Cocktail sauce for serving

Directions:

1. Preheat the grill to medium-high heat.
2. Toss the shrimp with olive oil, salt, and pepper in a bowl until evenly coated.
3. Thread the shrimp onto skewers, ensuring they are flat to prevent them from curling.
4. Place the shrimp skewers on the preheated grill and cook for about 2-3 minutes on each side until they turn pink and opaque.
5. Remove the shrimp from the grill and transfer them to a serving platter.
6. Serve the grilled shrimp with lemon wedges and cocktail sauce on the side.

Nutrition Facts:

- Serving Size: 1/4 of recipe
- Calories: 180
- Total Fat: 7g
- Saturated Fat: 1g
- Cholesterol: 220mg

- Sodium: 500mg
- Total Carbohydrates: 4g
- Dietary Fiber: 0g
- Sugars: 1g
- Protein: 24g

BACON-WRAPPED DATES

Prep Time: 15 minutes
Cooking Time: 20 minutes
Servings: 10
Ingredients:

- 20 whole dates, pitted
- 10 slices of bacon, cut in half
- 20 whole almonds (optional)
- Toothpicks

Directions:

1. Preheat your oven to 375°F (190°C). Line a baking sheet with parchment paper.
2. If using almonds, stuff each date with one almond.
3. Wrapping a half slice of bacon around each stuffed date, securing it with a toothpick.
4. Place the bacon-wrapped dates on the prepared baking sheet, seam side down.
5. Bake in the oven for 15-20 minutes or until the bacon is crispy and golden brown.
6. Remove from the oven and let cool slightly before serving.

Nutrition Facts (per serving):

- **Calories:** 120 kcal
- **Total Fat:** 6g
- **Saturated Fat:** 2g
- **Cholesterol:** 15mg
- **Sodium:** 220mg

- **Total Carbohydrates:** 12g
- **Dietary Fiber:** 1g
- **Sugars:** 10g
- **Protein:** 4g

TERIYAKI CHICKEN SKEWERS

Prep Time: 20 minutes
Cooking Time: 10 minutes
Servings: 4
Ingredients:

- 1 lb (450g) boneless, skinless chicken breasts, cut into 1-inch cubes
- 1/2 cup (120ml) soy sauce
- 1/4 cup (60ml) honey
- 2 cloves garlic, minced
- 1 tablespoon grated fresh ginger
- 2 tablespoons rice vinegar
- 1 tablespoon sesame oil
- 1 tablespoon cornstarch
- 2 tablespoons water
- Bamboo skewers, soaked in water for 30 minutes

Directions:

1. To make the teriyaki marinade, whisk together soy sauce, honey, garlic, ginger, rice vinegar, and sesame oil in a bowl.

2. Place the chicken cubes in a shallow dish or resealable plastic bag. Pour half of the teriyaki marinade over the chicken, reserving the other half for later. Make sure the chicken is well coated. Marinate for at least 15 minutes in the refrigerator or up to 2 hours for maximum flavour.

3. Preheat your grill or grill pan over medium-high heat.

4. Thread the marinated chicken cubes onto the soaked bamboo skewers.

5. In a small saucepan, mix the cornstarch and water until smooth. Stir in the reserved teriyaki marinade. Bring to a boil over medium heat, stirring constantly until the sauce thickens. Remove from heat and set aside.

6. Grill the chicken skewers for about 4-5 minutes on each side or until cooked through, basting occasionally with the thickened teriyaki sauce.

7. Once the chicken has a nice char, remove it from the grill and rest for a few minutes.

8. Serve the teriyaki chicken skewers hot, garnished with sesame seeds and chopped green onions if desired. Enjoy!

Nutrition Facts (per serving):

- Calories: 260
- Total Fat: 5g
- Saturated Fat: 1g
- Cholesterol: 80mg
- Sodium: 1220mg
- Total Carbohydrate: 20g
- Dietary Fiber: 0.5g
- Sugars: 17g
- Protein: 31g

GRILLED STUFFED JALAPENOS

Prep Time: 20 minutes
Cooking Time: 10 minutes
Servings: 6
Ingredients:

- 12 large jalapeño peppers
- 8 ounces cream cheese, softened
- 1 cup shredded cheddar cheese
- 1/4 cup finely chopped red onion
- 2 cloves garlic, minced
- 1 teaspoon ground cumin
- 1/2 teaspoon smoked paprika
- Salt and pepper to taste
- 6 slices bacon
- Toothpicks

Directions:

1. Preheat your grill to medium heat.

2. Cut the jalapeños in half lengthwise and remove the seeds and membranes. Do not touch your face or eyes while handling the peppers.

3. Combine the softened cream cheese, shredded cheddar cheese, chopped red onion, minced garlic, ground cumin, smoked paprika, salt, and pepper in a mixing bowl. Mix until well combined.

4. Spoon the cheese mixture into each jalapeño half, filling them evenly.

5. Wrap each stuffed jalapeño with a slice of bacon and secure it with a toothpick.

6. Place the stuffed jalapeños on the preheated grill and cook for about 5 minutes per side until the bacon is crispy and the peppers are tender.

7. Once cooked, remove the stuffed jalapeños from the grill and let them cool slightly before serving.

Nutrition Facts (per serving):

- Calories: 260
- Total Fat: 21g
- Saturated Fat: 11g
- Cholesterol: 59mg
- Sodium: 474mg
- Total Carbohydrates: 5g
- Dietary Fiber: 1g
- Sugars: 2g
- Protein: 12g

CAPRESE SALAD SKEWERS

- **Prep Time:** 15 minutes
- **Cooking Time:** 0 minutes
- **Servings:** 4

Ingredients:

- 16 cherry tomatoes
- 16 fresh mozzarella balls (bocconcini)

- 16 fresh basil leaves
- Balsamic glaze for drizzling
- Extra virgin olive oil for drizzling
- Salt and pepper to taste
- Wooden skewers

Directions:

1. Begin by washing the cherry tomatoes and basil leaves. Drain the mozzarella balls if they're stored in liquid.
2. Thread one cherry tomato onto each skewer, followed by a folded basil leaf and a mozzarella ball.
3. Repeat this process until all skewers are assembled.
4. Arrange the skewers on a serving platter.
5. Drizzle with balsamic glaze and extra virgin olive oil.
6. Season with salt and pepper to taste.
7. Serve immediately as a delightful appetizer or light snack.

Nutrition Facts (per serving):

- **Calories:** 180
- **Total Fat:** 12g
  - Saturated Fat: 5g
  - Trans Fat: 0g
- **Cholesterol:** 25mg
- **Sodium:** 280mg
- **Total Carbohydrates:** 5g
  - Dietary Fiber: 1g
  - Sugars: 3g
- **Protein:** 13g

BBQ MEATBALL SLIDERS

Prep Time: 15 minutes
Cooking Time: 20 minutes
Servings: 6
Ingredients:

- 1 pound ground beef

- 1/2 cup breadcrumbs
- 1/4 cup grated Parmesan cheese
- 1/4 cup milk
- 1 egg
- 1/4 cup chopped parsley
- 1 teaspoon garlic powder
- Salt and pepper to taste
- 1 cup BBQ sauce
- 12 slider buns
- Sliced cheese (optional)
- Sliced pickles (optional)
- Sliced onions (optional)

Directions:

1. Preheat your oven to 375°F (190°C).
2. Combine ground beef, breadcrumbs, Parmesan cheese, milk, egg, parsley, garlic powder, salt, and pepper in a large mixing bowl. Mix until well combined.
3. Shape the mixture into small meatballs about 1 inch in diameter.
4. Place the meatballs on a baking sheet lined with parchment paper and bake in the oven for 15-20 minutes or until cooked.
5. Once the meatballs are cooked, transfer them to a large bowl and pour BBQ sauce over them. Toss until the sauce is evenly coated.
6. Slice the slider buns horizontally and place a meatball on the bottom half of each bun.
7. Add optional toppings, such as sliced cheese, pickles, and onions.
8. Place the top half of the slider bun on each meatball to form a sandwich.
9. Serve immediately and enjoy!

Nutrition Facts (per serving):

- Calories: 380
- Total Fat: 15g
- Saturated Fat: 6g
- Cholesterol: 85mg

- Sodium: 780mg
- Total Carbohydrate: 37g
- Dietary Fiber: 2g
- Sugars: 14g
- Protein: 23g

GRILLED ARTICHOKE WITH GARLIC AIOLI

Prep Time: 15 minutes
Cooking Time: 25 minutes
Servings: 4
Ingredients:

- 4 large artichokes
- 2 lemons, halved
- 2 tablespoons olive oil
- Salt and pepper to taste

For the Garlic Aioli:

- 1 cup mayonnaise
- 2 cloves garlic, minced
- 1 tablespoon lemon juice
- Salt and pepper to taste

Directions:

1. **Prepare the Artichokes:** Trim the stem of each artichoke so they can stand upright. Cut off the top quarter of each artichoke. Use kitchen scissors to trim the sharp points from the remaining leaves. Rub the cut surfaces with lemon halves to prevent browning.

2. **Steam the Artichokes:** Place the artichokes in a steamer basket over boiling water. Squeeze the lemon halves over the artichokes and add them to the steamer basket. Cover and steam for about 20 minutes or until the leaves are tender and easily pulled off.

3. **Prepare the Grill:** Preheat the grill to medium-high heat.

4. **Grill the Artichokes:** Once steamed, remove them from the steamer basket and let them cool slightly. Cut each artichoke in half lengthwise. Brush the cut sides with olive oil and season with salt and pepper. Place

the artichokes on the preheated grill and cut the side down. Grill for about 5 minutes until char marks form.

5. **Make the Garlic Aioli:** In a small bowl, combine mayonnaise, minced garlic, lemon juice, salt, and pepper. Mix well until smooth and creamy. Adjust seasoning to taste.

6. **Serve:** Remove the grilled artichokes from the grill and arrange them on a serving platter. Serve hot with the garlic aioli on the side for dipping.

Nutrition Facts (per serving):

- Calories: 320
- Total Fat: 26g
- Saturated Fat: 4g
- Cholesterol: 15mg
- Sodium: 390mg
- Total Carbohydrate: 20g
- Dietary Fiber: 10g
- Sugars: 2g
- Protein: 5g

GREEK MEATBALLS WITH TZATZIKI

Prep Time: 20 minutes
Cooking Time: 20 minutes
Servings: 4
Ingredients:

- 1 pound ground lamb or beef
- 1/2 cup breadcrumbs
- 1/4 cup finely chopped red onion
- 2 cloves garlic, minced
- 1 teaspoon dried oregano
- 1 teaspoon dried mint
- 1/2 teaspoon ground cumin
- Salt and pepper to taste
- 1 tablespoon olive oil

For the Tzatziki:

- 1 cup Greek yogurt
- 1/2 cucumber, grated and squeezed to remove excess moisture
- 1 clove garlic, minced
- 1 tablespoon chopped fresh dill
- 1 tablespoon lemon juice
- Salt and pepper to taste

Directions:

1. **Preheat** the oven to 375°F (190°C). Line a baking sheet with parchment paper.
2. **Combine** the ground lamb or beef, breadcrumbs, red onion, minced garlic, oregano, mint, cumin, salt, and pepper in a large bowl. Mix until well combined.
3. **Shape** the mixture into meatballs about 1 inch in diameter.
4. **Heat** olive oil in a large skillet over medium heat. Add the meatballs in batches and cook until browned on all sides, about 2-3 minutes per side.
5. **Transfer** the browned meatballs to the prepared baking sheet and bake in the oven for 10-12 minutes or until cooked.
6. **While** the meatballs are baking, prepare the tzatziki. **Combine** the Greek yoghurt, grated cucumber, minced garlic, chopped dill, lemon juice, salt, and pepper in a bowl. Stir until well combined.
7. **Serve** the meatballs hot with tzatziki sauce on the side for dipping.

Nutrition Facts (per serving):

- Calories: 380
- Total Fat: 22g
- Saturated Fat: 9g
- Cholesterol: 85mg
- Sodium: 340mg
- Total Carbohydrate: 15g
- Dietary Fiber: 2g
- Sugars: 3g
- Protein: 28g

BRUSCHETTA WITH BALSAMIC GLAZE

Prep Time: 15 minutes
Cooking Time: 10 minutes
Servings: 4
Ingredients:

- 4 large ripe tomatoes, diced
- 1/4 cup fresh basil leaves, chopped
- 2 cloves garlic, minced
- 2 tablespoons extra virgin olive oil
- Salt and black pepper to taste
- 1 French baguette, sliced diagonally
- 1/2 cup balsamic vinegar
- 1 tablespoon brown sugar
- 1/4 cup shredded Parmesan cheese (optional)

Directions:

1. Preheat your oven to 400°F (200°C).
2. Combine the diced tomatoes, chopped basil, minced garlic, and extra virgin olive oil in a mixing bowl. Season with salt and pepper to taste. Set aside to let the flavours meld.
3. Place the baguette slices on a baking sheet and toast them in the oven for about 5 minutes or until lightly golden brown.
4. In a small saucepan, combine the balsamic vinegar and brown sugar. Bring to a simmer over medium heat, then reduce the heat to low. Let it simmer gently for about 5-7 minutes or until the vinegar has thickened to a glaze-like consistency. Remove from heat and allow to cool slightly.
5. Once the baguette slices are toasted, remove them from the oven and top each with the tomato mixture.
6. Drizzle the balsamic glaze over the topped baguette slices.
7. Optional: Sprinkle shredded Parmesan cheese over the bruschetta for added flavour.
8. Serve immediately and enjoy!

Nutrition Facts (per serving):

- Calories: 275
- Total Fat: 9g
- Saturated Fat: 2g
- Cholesterol: 4mg
- Sodium: 427mg
- Total Carbohydrate: 41g
- Dietary Fiber: 3g
- Sugars: 12g
- Protein: 7g

GRILLED POLENTA BITES WITH PESTO

Prep Time: 15 minutes
Cooking Time: 20 minutes
Servings: 4
Ingredients:

- 1 cup instant polenta
- 4 cups water
- Salt and pepper to taste
- 1 cup prepared pesto
- Olive oil for grilling
- Optional: grated Parmesan cheese for garnish

Directions:

1. **Prepare Polenta:** In a medium saucepan, bring water to a boil. Slowly pour in the instant polenta while whisking continuously to prevent lumps. Reduce heat to low and simmer, stirring frequently, until polenta thickens, about 5-7 minutes. Season with salt and pepper to taste.

2. **Pour and Set:** Pour the cooked polenta onto a baking sheet lined with parchment paper, spreading it evenly to about ½ inch thickness. Allow it to cool and set in the refrigerator for at least 30 minutes.

3. **Slice Polenta:** Once the polenta has set, use a knife to cut it into bite-sized squares or any desired shape.

4. **Preheat Grill:** Preheat your grill to medium-high heat. Brush the grill grates with olive oil to prevent sticking.

5. **Grill Polenta:** Carefully place the polenta slices onto the preheated grill. Cook for 3-4 minutes on each side or until grill marks form and the polenta is heated.

6. **Serve:** Remove the grilled polenta bites from the grill and arrange them on a serving platter. Top each bite with a dollop of prepared pesto. Optionally, sprinkle grated Parmesan cheese over the top for added flavour.

7. **Enjoy:** Serve immediately and enjoy these delicious grilled polenta bites with pesto as an appetizer or side dish!

Nutrition Facts:

- Serving Size: 1/4 of recipe
- Calories: 300
- Total Fat: 18g
- Saturated Fat: 3g
- Cholesterol: 0mg
- Sodium: 450mg
- Total Carbohydrates: 30g
- Dietary Fiber: 3g
- Sugars: 1g
- Protein: 5g

COCONUT SHRIMP WITH MANGO SALSA

Prep Time: 20 minutes
Cooking Time: 10 minutes
Servings: 4
Ingredients:
For the Coconut Shrimp:

- 1 pound large shrimp, peeled and deveined
- 1 cup all-purpose flour
- 2 eggs, beaten
- 1 cup shredded coconut
- 1 cup Panko breadcrumbs
- Salt and pepper to taste

- Vegetable oil for frying

For the Mango Salsa:

- 2 ripe mangoes, diced
- 1/2 red onion, finely chopped
- 1 red bell pepper, diced
- 1/4 cup fresh cilantro, chopped
- Juice of 1 lime
- Salt and pepper to taste

Directions:

1. **Prepare the Mango Salsa:** In a mixing bowl, combine diced mangoes, chopped red onion, diced red bell pepper, chopped cilantro, and lime juice. Season with salt and pepper to taste. Mix well and refrigerate until ready to serve.

2. **Prepare the Coconut Shrimp:** Pat the shrimp dry with paper towels and season with salt and pepper.

3. Set up three shallow dishes for dredging: one with flour, one with beaten eggs, and one with a mixture of shredded coconut and Panko breadcrumbs.

4. Dredge each shrimp in flour, dip them into the beaten eggs, and finally coat them with the coconut-Panko mixture, pressing gently to adhere.

5. In a large skillet, heat vegetable oil over medium-high heat. Fry the coated shrimp in batches for 2-3 minutes on each side or until golden brown and cooked through. Transfer to a paper towel-lined plate to drain excess oil.

6. Serve the coconut shrimp hot with the mango salsa on the side.

Nutrition Facts (per serving): NUTRITION FACTS MAY VARY DEPENDING ON SPECIFIC INGREDIENTS AND SERVING SIZES.

- Calories: 380
- Total Fat: 18g
- Saturated Fat: 12g
- Cholesterol: 265mg
- Sodium: 470mg
- Total Carbohydrate: 38g

- Dietary Fiber: 4g
- Sugars: 15g
- Protein: 20g

ANTIPASTO SKEWERS

- **Prep Time:** 20 minutes
- **Cooking Time:** 0 minutes
- **Servings:** 6

Ingredients:

- 12 cherry tomatoes
- 12 mozzarella balls
- 12 slices of salami
- 12 slices of prosciutto
- 1/2 cup black olives
- 1/2 cup green olives
- 1/4 cup balsamic glaze
- 1 tablespoon olive oil
- Salt and pepper to taste
- Fresh basil leaves for garnish

Directions:

1. Start by assembling your skewers. Take a skewer and thread on a cherry tomato, followed by a mozzarella ball, a slice of salami folded into quarters, a prosciutto folded into quarters, and an olive. Repeat until all ingredients are used, making 12 skewers in total.

2. Arrange the assembled skewers on a serving platter.

3. In a small bowl, whisk together the balsamic glaze and olive oil. Drizzle this mixture over the skewers.

4. Season the skewers with salt and pepper to taste.

5. Garnish with fresh basil leaves.

6. Serve immediately and enjoy your delicious antipasto skewers!

Nutrition Facts (per serving):

- Calories: 220

- Total Fat: 16g
- Saturated Fat: 6g
- Cholesterol: 30mg
- Sodium: 550mg
- Total Carbohydrates: 6g
- Dietary Fiber: 2g
- Sugars: 3g
- Protein: 14g

Bacon-Wrapped Scallops
Prep Time: 15 minutes
Cooking Time: 15 minutes
Servings: 4
Ingredients:

- 12 large sea scallops, patted dry
- 12 slices of bacon, cut in half
- Salt and pepper to taste
- Toothpicks or skewers
- 2 tablespoons olive oil
- 1 tablespoon chopped fresh parsley (optional, for garnish)
- Lemon wedges (for serving)

Directions:

1. Preheat your oven to 400°F (200°C). Line a baking sheet with parchment paper or aluminium foil for easy cleanup.
2. Season each scallop with salt and pepper to taste.
3. Wrapping each half slice of bacon around a scallop, securing it with a toothpick or skewer. Repeat until all scallops are wrapped.
4. Heat olive oil in a large skillet over medium-high heat. Once hot, add the bacon-wrapped scallops in batches, ensuring not to overcrowd the skillet. Cook for 2-3 minutes on each side until the bacon is browned and crispy.

5. Transfer the partially cooked scallops to the prepared baking sheet and finish cooking them in the preheated oven for about 5-7 minutes or until the scallops are opaque and cooked through.

6. Once cooked, remove the toothpicks or skewers from the scallops and transfer them to a serving platter.

7. Garnish with chopped parsley if desired, and serve hot with lemon wedges.

Nutrition Facts (per serving):

- Calories: 289 kcal
- Total Fat: 17g
  - Saturated Fat: 5g
  - Trans Fat: 0g
- Cholesterol: 58mg
- Sodium: 816mg
- Total Carbohydrate: 2g
  - Dietary Fiber: 0g
  - Sugars: 0g
- Protein: 30g

GRILLED STUFFED MUSHROOMS

Prep Time: 20 minutes
Cooking Time: 15 minutes
Servings: 4
Ingredients:

- 16 large mushrooms, stems removed and reserved
- 1 tablespoon olive oil
- 2 cloves garlic, minced
- 1 small onion, finely chopped
- 1/2 cup breadcrumbs
- 1/4 cup grated Parmesan cheese
- 2 tablespoons chopped fresh parsley
- Salt and pepper to taste
- Cooking spray

Directions:

1. Preheat the grill to medium heat.

2. Clean mushrooms and remove stems. Finely chop the stems and set aside.

3. Heat olive oil in a skillet over medium heat. Add minced garlic and chopped onion, and sauté until softened for about 3-4 minutes.

4. Add chopped mushroom stems to the skillet and cook for 2 minutes.

5. Remove skillet from heat and stir in breadcrumbs, Parmesan cheese, chopped parsley, salt, and pepper. The mixture should be moist enough to hold together.

6. Spoon the filling into the mushroom caps, pressing down gently to pack the filling.

7. Lightly coat the grill grates with cooking spray to prevent sticking.

8. Place the stuffed mushrooms on the grill, cover, and cook for 8-10 minutes, or until the mushrooms are tender and the filling is golden brown.

9. Serve hot and enjoy!

Nutrition Facts (per serving):

- **Calories:** 150
- **Total Fat:** 7g
- **Saturated Fat:** 2g
- **Cholesterol:** 5mg
- **Sodium:** 250mg
- **Total Carbohydrates:** 17g
- **Dietary Fiber:** 3g
- **Sugars:** 3g
- **Protein:** 6g

GRILLED VEGETABLE PLATTER WITH DIPPING SAUCE

Prep Time: 15 minutes
Cooking Time: 15 minutes
Servings: 4
Ingredients:

For the Grilled Vegetables:
- 1 red bell pepper, seeded and cut into strips
- 1 yellow bell pepper, seeded and cut into strips
- 1 zucchini, sliced into rounds
- 1 yellow squash, sliced into rounds
- 1 eggplant, sliced into rounds
- 8-10 cherry tomatoes
- 2 tablespoons olive oil
- Salt and pepper to taste
- 1 tablespoon chopped fresh herbs (such as basil, thyme, or rosemary)

For the Dipping Sauce:
- 1/2 cup plain Greek yogurt
- 1 tablespoon lemon juice
- 1 garlic clove, minced
- 1 tablespoon chopped fresh parsley
- Salt and pepper to taste

Directions:
1. **Prepare the Grilled Vegetables:** Preheat your grill to medium-high heat. In a large bowl, toss the bell peppers, zucchini, yellow squash, eggplant, and cherry tomatoes with olive oil, salt, pepper, and chopped herbs until well coated.
2. **Grill the Vegetables:** Place the vegetables directly on the grill grates or in a grill basket. Grill for about 4-5 minutes per side or until they are tender and have grill marks. Remove from the grill and transfer to a serving platter.
3. **Make the Dipping Sauce:** In a small bowl, combine the Greek yoghurt, lemon juice, minced garlic, chopped parsley, salt, and pepper. Stir until well mixed.
4. **Serve:** Arrange the grilled vegetables on a platter and serve with the dipping sauce on the side.

Nutrition Facts (per serving):
- Calories: 150
- Total Fat: 8g

- Saturated Fat: 1g
- Cholesterol: 3mg
- Sodium: 35mg
- Total Carbohydrate: 15g
- Dietary Fiber: 5g
- Sugars: 7g
- Protein: 7g

PROSCIUTTO-WRAPPED ASPARAGUS

Prep Time: 15 minutes
Cooking Time: 10 minutes
Servings: 4
Ingredients:

- 1 bunch of asparagus spears, tough ends trimmed
- 8 slices of prosciutto
- 2 tablespoons olive oil
- Salt and black pepper to taste
- Lemon wedges for serving (optional)

Directions:

1. Preheat your oven to 400°F (200°C).
2. Divide the asparagus spears into 8 equal bundles.
3. Take a slice of prosciutto and wrap it around each bundle of asparagus, starting at the bottom and spiralling upwards. Repeat for all bundles.
4. Place the wrapped asparagus bundles on a baking sheet lined with parchment paper.
5. Drizzle olive oil over the bundles and season with salt and black pepper.
6. Roast in the oven for 10 minutes or until the asparagus is tender and the prosciutto is crispy.
7. Remove from the oven and serve hot, optionally, with lemon wedges on the side.

Nutrition Facts (per serving):

- **Calories:** 135 kcal

- **Fat:** 9g
- **Saturated Fat:** 2g
- **Cholesterol:** 16mg
- **Sodium:** 455mg
- **Carbohydrates:** 5g
- **Fiber:** 2g
- **Sugar:** 2g
- **Protein:** 9g

BBQ CHICKEN FLATBREAD BITES

Prep Time: 15 minutes
Cooking Time: 15 minutes
Servings: 4-6
Ingredients:

- 2 flatbreads (store-bought or homemade)
- 1 cup cooked and shredded chicken breast
- 1/2 cup barbecue sauce
- 1/2 cup shredded mozzarella cheese
- 1/4 cup diced red onion
- 1/4 cup diced bell pepper (any colour)
- 2 tablespoons chopped fresh cilantro (optional)
- Olive oil for brushing

Directions:

1. Preheat your oven to 400°F (200°C).
2. Cut the flatbreads into bite-sized squares or triangles and place them on a baking sheet lined with parchment paper.
3. In a small bowl, toss the shredded chicken with barbecue sauce until evenly coated.
4. Spread the barbecue chicken evenly over the flatbread pieces.
5. Sprinkle shredded mozzarella cheese over the barbecue chicken.
6. Scatter diced red onion and bell pepper over the cheese.

7. Brush the edges of the flatbread with olive oil to help them crisp up in the oven.

8. Bake in the preheated oven for 12-15 minutes or until the cheese is melted and bubbly and the edges of the flatbread are crispy.

9. Once out of the oven, sprinkle chopped cilantro over the flatbread bites for a fresh finish.

10. Serve hot and enjoy!

Nutrition Facts:

- SERVING SIZE: 1/4 of the recipe
- CALORIES: 220
- TOTAL FAT: 7g
- SATURATED FAT: 2g
- CHOLESTEROL: 30mg
- SODIUM: 450mg
- TOTAL CARBOHYDRATES: 26g
- DIETARY FIBER: 1g
- SUGARS: 10g
- PROTEIN: 13g

GRILLED BRIE WITH CRANBERRY CHUTNEY

Prep Time: 10 minutes
Cooking Time: 10 minutes
Servings: 4
Ingredients:

- 1 wheel of Brie cheese (about 8 ounces)
- 1 cup cranberries (fresh or frozen)
- 1/4 cup orange juice
- 2 tablespoons honey
- 1 teaspoon grated fresh ginger
- 1/4 teaspoon ground cinnamon
- 1/4 teaspoon ground nutmeg
- Sliced baguette or crackers for serving

Directions:

1. Preheat your grill to medium-high heat.

2. Combine the cranberries, orange juice, honey, grated ginger, cinnamon, and nutmeg in a small saucepan. Cook over medium heat, stirring occasionally, until the cranberries burst and the mixture thickens slightly, about 5-7 minutes. Remove from heat and let cool slightly.

3. While the chutney is cooling, slice the Brie cheese into 1/2-inch slices.

4. Place the Brie slices directly on the grill grate and grill for 1-2 minutes per side or until the cheese is softened and has grill marks.

5. Remove the grilled Brie from the grill and transfer to a serving plate.

6. Spoon the cranberry chutney over the grilled Brie.

7. Serve immediately with sliced baguette or crackers.

Nutrition Facts (per serving):

- Calories: 250
- Total Fat: 15g
- Saturated Fat: 9g
- Cholesterol: 50mg
- Sodium: 300mg
- Total Carbohydrate: 20g
- Dietary Fiber: 1g
- Sugars: 15g
- Protein: 10g

TERIYAKI BEEF LETTUCE WRAPS

Prep Time: 15 minutes
Cooking Time: 15 minutes
Servings: 4
Ingredients:

- 1 lb (450g) lean beef, thinly sliced
- 1/2 cup teriyaki sauce
- 2 tablespoons soy sauce
- 1 tablespoon sesame oil

- 2 cloves garlic, minced
- 1 teaspoon ginger, grated
- 1 tablespoon brown sugar
- 1 tablespoon cornstarch
- 2 tablespoons water
- 1 head iceberg or butter lettuce, leaves separated
- 1/2 cup shredded carrots
- 1/2 cup sliced cucumber
- 1/4 cup chopped green onions
- Sesame seeds, for garnish
- Optional: Sriracha sauce for extra heat

Directions:

1. Mix teriyaki sauce, soy sauce, sesame oil, garlic, ginger, and brown sugar in a small bowl.
2. In a separate bowl, mix cornstarch and water to create a slurry.
3. Heat a skillet over medium-high heat. Add the beef slices and cook until browned, about 2-3 minutes.
4. Pour the teriyaki sauce mixture over the beef. Stir well to coat.
5. Add the cornstarch slurry to the skillet, stirring continuously until the sauce thickens, about 1-2 minutes. Remove from heat.
6. Arrange lettuce leaves on a serving platter. Spoon some beef onto each lettuce leaf.
7. Top with shredded carrots, sliced cucumber, and chopped green onions.
8. Garnish with sesame seeds and drizzle with Sriracha sauce if desired.
9. Serve immediately and enjoy!

Nutrition Facts (per serving):

- Calories: 290
- Total Fat: 12g
- Saturated Fat: 4g
- Cholesterol: 70mg
- Sodium: 1050mg

- Total Carbohydrate: 16g
- Dietary Fiber: 2g
- Sugars: 9g
- Protein: 28g

CRAB STUFFED AVOCADO HALVES

Prep Time: 15 minutes
Cooking Time: 0 minutes
Servings: 4
Ingredients:

- 2 ripe avocados
- 1 cup cooked crab meat, shredded
- 1/4 cup red bell pepper, diced
- 1/4 cup celery, diced
- 2 tablespoons red onion, finely chopped
- 2 tablespoons mayonnaise
- 1 tablespoon lemon juice
- 1 teaspoon Dijon mustard
- Salt and pepper to taste
- Chopped parsley or chives for garnish (optional)

Directions:

1. Cut the avocados in half lengthwise and remove the pits. Use a spoon to carefully scoop out some of the flesh from each avocado half, creating a larger cavity for the stuffing. Place the scooped avocado flesh in a mixing bowl and set the halves aside.

2. To the mixing bowl with the avocado flesh, add the shredded crab meat, diced red bell pepper, diced celery, finely chopped red onion, mayonnaise, lemon juice, Dijon mustard, salt, and pepper. Gently mix until all ingredients are well combined.

3. Taste the crab mixture and adjust the seasoning if needed.

4. Spoon the crab mixture into the cavities of the avocado halves, dividing it equally among them.